OUR JOURNEY HOME

Also by Jean Vanier

A Door of Hope
Jesus, the Gift of Love

Our Journey Home

*Rediscovering a common humanity
beyond our differences*

Jean Vanier

Translated by Maggie Parham

Novalis / Orbis

Our Journey Home: Rediscovering a Common Humanity Beyond Our Differences is published in Canada by Novalis Publishing, in England by Hodder and Stoughton, and in the U.S. by Orbis Books. First published by Librairie Plon in France as *Toute personne est une histoire sacrée.*

© Jean Vanier 1997

Hodder and Stoughton Ltd.
A Division of Hodder Headline PLC, 338 Euston Road, London NW13BH

British Library Cataloguing-in-Publication Data
A record for this book is available from the British Library.
ISBN: 0-340-66143-7

Orbis Books
Maryknoll, New York, U.S.A.

Library of Congress Catalogue Card No.: 96-49053
ISBN: 1-57075-117-X

Novalis Editorial Offices
Saint Paul University, 223 Main St., Ottawa, Ontario, Canada K1S 1C4

Novalis Business Offices
49 Front St. East, 2nd Floor, Toronto, Ontario, Canada M5E 1B3

Canadian Cataloguing-in-Publication Data

Vanier, Jean, 1928–
          Our journey home: rediscovering a common humanity
beyond our differences

Originally published in French under the title: Toute
          personne est une histoire sacrée.

ISBN 2-89088-867-3

          1. Philosophical anthropology. 2. Man. 3. Life.
4. Humanism. 5. Vanier, Jean, 1928– I. Title.

BD450.V2713   1997   128   C97-900016-5

Printed in Canada

Contents

Introduction

For more than thirty years I have lived in 'l'Arche' with men and women who have a mental handicap. Before this I was a naval officer and a professor of philosophy. The adventure of l'Arche began in 1963 when a Dominican priest, Father Thomas Philippe, invited me to visit Trosly-Breuil, a little village near Compiègne, about one hundred kilometres north of Paris. He wanted me to meet some new friends of his, people with mental handicaps who were living in a home where he was chaplain. I came and, feeling rather self-conscious and a little apprehensive, I met these men who in so many ways were weak and powerless. Accidents or sickness had caused them pain and suffering, but they had been wounded even more deeply by the contempt and rejection they had known. My visit moved me very much. Each of the men I met seemed starved of friendship and affection; each one clung to me, asking, through words or gestures: 'Do you love me? Do you want to be my friend?' And each one demanded, through his damaged and broken body: 'Why? Why am I like this? Why do my parents not want me? Why can't I be like my brothers and sisters who are married?'

Through this first meeting, I entered into a world of suffering of which I had previously known nothing. Touched by the questions these men put to me, I began to visit psychiatric hospitals, institutions and asylums. I also met parents whose children had a mental handicap. Gradually, I

discovered their intense suffering, and the enormous scale of the problem. When I visited mental hospitals in those days, I would often find hundreds of men and women turning aimlessly round and round. Their expressions were full of despair, and yet their faces lit up when they were treated as human beings. All this completely changed my life.

In an asylum near Paris I met two men with mental handicaps, Raphael Simi and Philippe Seux. Raphael had had meningitis when he was young, and this had left him almost unable to talk, and unable to move freely. Philippe could talk, but encephalitis had left one of his legs and one of his arms paralysed. After the death of their parents, without anyone asking them what they felt about it, both men had been placed in this asylum. My first step was to buy a small and rather dilapidated house in Trosly and, having obtained the necessary permission from the local authorities, I invited Raphael and Philippe to come and live with me.

And so in August 1964, l'Arche was born. We lived together. We did everything together: cooking, housework, gardening, going for walks. I gradually became aware of how deeply these men had suffered, particularly of the pain they had endured through having always been regarded by their parents and by everyone around them as a disappointment, and through never having been appreciated or seen as having value as human beings. I began to understand that what they longed for was to have friends and to live, as far as possible, like other people.

Everywhere, there was prejudice against them. Some people avoided them, others pitied them. Most often, people regarded them with contempt. A great wall separated them from those to whom we apply that terrible term 'normal people'. I began to realise that there were prejudices at work within me too: I was not listening to Raphael and Philippe enough. Little by little, I came to understand that

I must have more respect for their freedom and allow them to make choices.

I called the community l'Arche (the Ark) after Noah's ark, which saved humanity from the flood. The community of l'Arche wants to provide a refuge for people with mental handicaps, who can so quickly be drowned in the waters of our competitive society.

My friendship with Raphael and Philippe deepened. We were happy together. There were times of sharing, real celebrations. The rhythm of our lives was simple. We had our work in the house and garden (and later on in the workshops), and our meals together were often full of joy. We shared times of fun and relaxation and also of prayer. As far as I was concerned, Raphael and Philippe were not so much men with mental handicaps as friends. It did me good to be with them, and I think it did them good to be with me. Others came to join us. We were able to welcome more people with mental handicaps. L'Arche began to grow.

Today, there are nearly four hundred of us in this first community: two hundred people with handicaps and two hundred assistants. We live together in about twenty houses spread across five villages. We work in the gardens and in a number of workshops. About thirty of the people with mental handicaps live with their families and come to work with us. Some assistants are single, some married. Roughly half of them are with l'Arche on a permanent basis; the rest come here for periods of anything from three months to three years.

Out of this first community at Trosly, over one hundred other l'Arche communities have grown. They are spread across twenty-six countries, in each of the five continents. All of us adhere to the same charter, which defines our aims and the spirit and purpose of our community life.

People with handicaps and assistants live together in houses integrated into the life either of a village or a town. We form a new type of family or community where the strong help the weak, and the weak help the strong.

In 1971, the first Faith and Light communities were formed. Marie-Hélène Mathieu and I, together with some friends, organised an international pilgrimage to Lourdes for people with mental handicaps, their parents and their friends. Altogether, there were twelve thousand pilgrims. It was a time of immense joy for all of us, but above all for the many parents who had suffered the grief of having sons or daughters who were excluded from society. Faith and Light grew out of this pilgrimage. Today, in seventy countries, there are more than one thousand three hundred Faith and Light communities. Each is made up of about thirty people: people with handicaps, their families and their friends. The members of these communities do not live together but they meet regularly, at least once a month, to share their sufferings and their joys, to celebrate together and to pray. In their different ways, the l'Arche communities and those of Faith and Light are centred on the person with disabilities, who is seen in the fullness of his or her humanity, capable not only of receiving from others but also of giving to them.

And here we touch on the paradox of l'Arche and of Faith and Light, a paradox which is at the heart of this book. People with mental handicaps, so limited physically and intellectually, are often more gifted than others when it comes to the things of the heart and to relationships. In a mysterious way they can lead us to the home of our hearts. Their intellectual handicaps are counterbalanced by a special openness and trust in others. Certain social conventions and ideas about what is important mean nothing to them. They live closer to what really matters.

In our competitive societies, which put so much emphasis on power and strength, they have great difficulty in finding their place; they are losers in every competition. But in their thirst and their gift for friendship and for communion, the weaker people in society can touch and transform the strong, if the strong are only prepared to listen to them. In our fragmented, often broken societies, in our towns made of steel and glass and loneliness, people with disabilities can act as a kind of cement that binds people together. This is their role in society. They have a special part to play in the healing of hearts and in destroying the barriers which separate people from one another and prevent them from living happily and humanly.

I have called this book 'Our Journey Home' because I believe that the danger for us human beings is to sacrifice humaneness and solidarity in order to reach up to the skies. This has led humanity to continual competition and to warfare. We are all fighting to be the winners. Today, though, warfare is too dangerous and we are now more than ever painfully aware of all that is broken in our universe. To save our planet, to save humanity, must we not come back down to earth? Not only to find again the beautiful harmony of our earth, but also the home of our bodies, the home of our hearts.

Home is where we are safe. It is no longer a question of competition, for home is a place of communion. 'Going home' is a journey to the heart of who we are, a place where we can be ourselves and welcome the reality of our beauty and our pain. From this acceptance of ourselves, we can accept others as they are and we can see our common humanity.

My experience is that people with handicaps have brought me home to myself, to all that is broken within me. And from this has developed a better acceptance of others as they are, with all that is wounded in them. Through community, which is a body of people, they have helped me to discover that human beings can be 'at home' with each other. Is this not the journey that we should all be taking, but have somehow lost our way?

If we are really to understand the important and paradoxical role of people with handicaps it seems to me necessary to have some experience. Words and theories are not enough. The things that I suggest may seem naive, utopian; they may even seem a way of trying to make sense of difficult lives, of finding meaning where there is none. But these are not just words. These are things that I have learned by living.

This is not to say that life at l'Arche is easy and straightforward. Far from it! It is sometimes tough and demanding. We must not be idealistic about people with mental handicaps. Some have been victims of so much contempt and violence, which they have stored up inside themselves, that there can be an explosion of violence, especially when they first come to live in a l'Arche community. Anger and depression remain with certain people with a mental handicap for the whole of their lives. At l'Arche, there are moments of elation, but there are also moments of great pain and anguish.

But for the people living with them, there is a positive side to these difficulties. They reveal our limitations, our vulnerabilities, our need to be reassured and understood, our blindness, our blockages, all those things which we hid from ourselves and from others before coming to l'Arche. When you live a life of fairly intense relationships, in a community, you quickly discover who you are. It is impossible to hide anything. If in every person's heart there is a thirst for communion and friendship, there are also deep wounds, fears and a whole world of darkness which govern our lives in a hidden way. Coming to know this shadow side, and then to accept it, seems to me to be a first step towards true self-knowledge.

At l'Arche, we seek to restore to people with handicaps their own particular humanity, the humanity which has effectively been stolen from them. In order to do this, it is necessary to create a warm, family environment in which people are able to develop according to their potential, to live as happily as possible, and to become truly themselves. It is as if in l'Arche they can refind their journey home.

If people come to us deeply disturbed, they need to be supported by psychologists and psychiatrists. Right from the beginning of l'Arche, I found competent men and women who helped me to reflect on the needs of people with handicaps. Through experience, I have gained quite a lot of knowledge of psychology and psychopathology. All this has opened up new horizons for me.

Father Thomas Philippe, the priest who first invited me to Trosly in 1963, stayed at the heart of l'Arche for twenty-eight years. He was like a gentle and humble representative of God among us, full of compassion for all the members of the community, above all for those who were weakest and suffered most. He was close to each of us, and the spiritual director of many. He who had been for many years a professor of theology and philosophy had absorbed the full truth of St Paul's words: 'God has chosen that which is foolish in the world to confound the wise, and that which is weak to confound the strong. He has chosen those of low birth and those who are despised' (1 Cor. 1:27–8). People with mental handicaps, usually incapable of abstract thought, are often more able to welcome the presence of others. Less competitive, they are better at creating communion. Father Thomas saw immediately that this hidden capacity made them more open to welcoming the presence of the God of love.

Life at l'Arche has been, and is, a profound experience for me, both humanly and spiritually. It has made me understand how the Gospels really are good news for the poor, and how psychology and psychiatry can help people in difficulty to regain their equilibrium, especially if they live in a truly human environment.

People with mental handicaps led me into the immense joy of communion but also into the terrible pain and fears that come up as we let down our barriers and become vulnerable to others. They led me to the discovery of my immense need for Jesus. I am still on this journey through tenderness and pain towards wholeness and union with others and with God.

Since 1980, I have ceased to be the director of the community; my role has changed. I still live in a house with people who have disabilities, but I spend a lot of my time accompanying assistants, listening to them and helping them to understand the meaning of all that they are living. If I haven't read many books on psychology, I have learned from listening to others. My understanding of human beings, their call to grow so that they become fully themselves and overcome their fears, has developed through this listening.

I also spend time helping l'Arche and Faith and Light communities to come into being and to grow in maturity in different countries, especially the countries which are poorest. For many people, the vision which inspires these communities is completely new. Parents of children with handicaps are often amazed to discover that their son's or daughter's life has meaning, that he or she has a place in society and something to give to others.

I have been privileged to get to know a great many

cultures and different religions, and to see the beauty in each one. All this has helped me to discover the meaning of our common humanity, and the preciousness of each individual human being.

I am a disciple of Jesus and I seek to live my life by the light of the Gospel. Born a Catholic, I am nourished by the church in which I have my roots. I love this church. I know, of course, that it has its shortcomings – the same shortcomings as the people within the church. Following Jesus in an authentic way is difficult. Yet through community life in l'Arche and Faith and Light, I have also discovered the beauty and truth reflected in disciples of Jesus who are members of other Christian churches, and in people who belong to other religions, or who have no religion at all.

In this book I would like to share the essentials of what I have learned since l'Arche began. It is a book of anthropology, focussing on what it is to be human. For we all share a common humanity, whatever our culture or faith, our gifts or handicaps. It is this common humanity that I want to talk about, not from a theoretical point of view, but from my experiences of the last thirty years.

My studies in Aristotle helped me to order my thoughts, and to distinguish what really matters from what is less important. Aristotle loved all that is human. He made me pay attention not primarily to ideas but to reality and experience. But I differ from Aristotle over certain aspects of anthropology, particularly over his definition of the human being as 'a rational animal', a definition which excludes people with mental handicaps from humanity. I would sooner define the human being as 'someone capable of love'.

Father Thomas was not only my spiritual director, he was also my intellectual teacher. He was rooted in the thinking of St Thomas Aquinas, but at the same time had great respect for the human sciences. Two psychiatrists, Dr Thompson and Dr Préaut, had opened his eyes to the crucial importance of the relationship between a mother and her child in the development of a human being's emotional life. Father Thomas considered this relationship, on which our ability to form other relationships is founded, essential in understanding the life of faith and the spiritual life. He helped me thus to put communion at the heart of my thinking about human beings.*

I am now moving into old age, the last stage of my life. This is a book of reflection rather than an autobiography. If I were to write an autobiography – to move through my life chronologically describing the things that have happened to me and the people I have met – it would not be possible to explain the purpose and meaning of my life. I prefer to write, very simply, about what life has taught me and about what I believe and about my own journey home. In doing this I hope I can help those who are searching, those who suffer and those who seek to love.

---

* cf. His leaflets on *The Stages of Life* (Saint Paul, Paris, 1994).

A question of language

Language has evolved a great deal over the last thirty years. People used to talk about the 'mentally retarded' or the 'mentally deficient'. Today we use other terms: 'people with learning disabilities' or 'people who are mentally challenged'. Language evolves according to culture, country and times. Behind the change of language is the desire to affirm that a person with a mental handicap is first and foremost *a person*, who should be respected and given the opportunity to exercise his or her particular gifts.

In this book, I have kept the term 'a person with a mental handicap' or 'people with mental handicaps'. They are truly *people* with all the implications that this word holds. Each person is unique and important. Yet there is difference. Some people come, or are sent, to L'Arche because of their handicap; others choose freely to come and live with them. The important thing is to signify difference while respecting the person.

Sometimes today people have difficulty with the words 'the poor' and 'the weak'. The gospel message talks about 'the poor' and this is frequently interpreted as the 'economically poor'. But a person without work and a parent who has lost a child are also poor. The poor person is one who is in need, who recognises this need and cries out for help. Weakness is frequently considered a defect. But are we not all weak and needy in some way? We all have our vulnerable points, our limits and our handicaps. When we recognise our weaknesses, we can ask for help; we can work together. The weak need the strong but, as we are discovering in l'Arche, the strong also need the weak. In this book I have occasionally used the words 'poor' and 'weak', even though they go against certain cultural norms that want everyone to be strong.

Special thanks

I am grateful to Maggie Parham for having worked hard on this translation and Alison Bell for having reworked the text with great competence. In point of fact, it is more than a translation because in working on the English text, I felt free enough to render more precise my thought and even to add things that were not in the French text.

I

THE WALLS

When I first encountered people with mental handicaps, I began to discover that society is governed by walls, walls which shut people in, walls which prevent people from meeting and talking to others. The first walls I came across were those of the pyschiatric hospitals and institutions that I visited. Raphael and Philippe were both hidden behind thick walls. I invited them to come and live with me in the little house that I called l'Arche, in the village of Trosly. The house looked straight out on to the road, without even a garden or garden walls to separate us from passers-by. Raphael and Philippe inspired fear in some of the villagers, and an unhealthy pity in others. Sometimes, people told me I was 'marvellous' because I was devoting my life to people 'like that'. The more my friendship with these two men grew, the more wounded I felt by such attitudes and remarks. Gradually, I learned how our society rejected men and women with mental handicaps, regarding them as nature's mistakes, as sub-human. There was a kind of pyschological barrier which stood in the way of their being regarded as human beings. Sometimes I detected these barriers within myself, when I failed to listen properly to Raphael and Philippe.

In 1964, when l'Arche began, there were still many people with mental handicaps hidden away by their parents. Even their neighbours did not know of their existence. I once came across a teenager on a farm chained up in a garage.

3

Many were shut away in homes, psychiatric hospitals and squalid institutions. In some hospitals I discovered wards crammed with men and women who were treated and talked about as if they were vegetables.

Walls surrounded not only the people with handicaps but also their parents who felt guilty, or even punished by God. Many felt themselves excluded from the church because of their child, who made too much noise and disrupted the services. In those days, people with mental handicaps were not allowed to receive Holy Communion. They were often called mentally deficient. They were part of another world, a world without human worth, a world of misfits.

One day, a father came to my house to visit his son. In the middle of lunch, someone happened to comment to him and his son: 'You two have the same eyes.' The father, an industrialist, snapped back aggressively, 'No, he has his mother's eyes.' What he was really saying was, 'There is absolutely no likeness between my son and myself.' This brutal remark, spontaneous and swift, cut his son to the quick, and as soon as the meal was over he fled from the room. The father asked me where he had gone. He had not realised how much he had hurt his son. I am sure he believed he really had learned to accept him, but in fact he remained very wounded by having had a son who had a mental handicap. He had not managed to accept him, and felt ashamed of him.

Another day, a sad though perfectly 'normal' man came to see me. He was sitting in my study telling me about his domestic, professional and financial trials and tribulations. Somebody knocked on my door and before I had time to answer, Jean-Claude came in. Some people would describe Jean-Claude as a mongol, others would say that he had Down's syndrome. To us, he is just Jean-Claude. He is a relaxed, happy, cheerful man (even if he does not much like working!). He took my hand and said hello. Then he took 'Mr Normal's' hand and said hello, and left the room laughing. 'Mr Normal' then turned to me and said: 'How sad it is to see people like that!' In fact, what was sad was that 'Mr Normal' was blinded by his prejudices and by his own unhappiness. He seemed unable to see Jean-Claude's beauty, laughter and joy. There was a sort of psychological barrier between them.

Certainly, some cultures are more open to those who are weak. But I have come across others completely contemptuous of their weaker members: people mock, abuse, reject and maltreat them; they shun them, or sometimes just leave them to die. I have seen dreadful, rat-infested homes where half-naked men and women turn round and round looking as if they might die of sadness. Some institutions are hidden away miles from the nearest town, practically inaccessible to the families of the people living in them. These are the walls behind which society hides those it considers undesirable. In psychiatric institutions, I have seen locked rooms in which thirty-odd completely naked men were just waiting to die.

People with mental handicaps, and above all those with severe handicaps, are among the most rejected members of our society. The French government has recently passed a law forbidding discrimination against people with mental handicaps. This is a good move. But France has also brought in a law to say that a baby diagnosed as having a handicap can be aborted at any point during the mother's pregnancy. For other babies, abortion is only permitted during the first fifteen weeks after conception. At school, if a child wants to insult a classmate, he calls him a 'spastic'. Most young women cannot bear the idea of being pregnant with 'a monster' (this is a word often used in France for people with handicaps), and insist that if they ever found themselves in that position, they would have an abortion. Despite the fact that some young people really stand up for them, I find that among many others, rejection of people with handicaps is becoming stronger. Maybe today there is more acceptance of people with handicaps, but there is also more violence towards them.

In certain countries, we have seen the development of special schools, or sometimes integrated schools and work-shops for people with handicaps. There has been a move towards emptying the huge institutions and psychiatric hospitals. But many of the people who have supposedly been taken back into society find themselves alone, lost in huge towns, imprisoned in their sadness without any kind of community. The physical walls may have disappeared, but the psychological walls remain.

These walls built around people with mental handicaps are only the most visible of the great walls that we build to keep ourselves separated from other people.

The wall between the strong and the weak

Weakness gives rise to fear. Isn't that what we see so often with old people, when they feel their strength diminishing? Feelings of anger, rebellion and depression begin to well up in them. They no longer attract people through their charm and their *joie de vivre*; on the contrary, depression makes meetings painful. Their children dread coming to see them, because their parents have become so critical and aggressive. The old people are acutely aware of their aggression, and their lack of joy and peace. But this awareness only serves to increase their depression. They feel they are a burden to their children and that they have no more reason to live, and they risk cutting themselves off from others in their unhappiness.

The transition from being strong and active to being weak, dependent and no longer capable of action is not an easy one. I will speak about it at greater length in the chapter on the stages of life. The transition implies important changes in lifestyle, and it is particularly difficult for the person who has always striven to appear strong, to have power, important positions and privileges in society, to be admired and to better themselves socially and professionally. Weakness for somebody like this is failure. No longer having a position or occupation recognised and respected by others uncovers a void at the centre of their being. This void breeds anguish and a lack of self-confidence; then guilt takes hold. The person feels totally useless. From the top of a pedestal and the peak of success, we can quickly fall into the pit. Having been elated and self-satisfied, we can quickly become engulfed in the depths of depression, rebellion and despair.

Isn't this why in our societies, where strength and success are often considered paramount, we find ourselves needing to build more and more homes and hospices for old people? People cannot bear to have old people living with them; they find them unsettling. Certainly many families do not have enough space to take them in, or they do not want to create it. Some of the homes for old people are dismal. They are filled with apathy, and the pensioners living in them are bored to death. There are no organised activities and few people visit them.

In poorer countries, old people are revered. There is no question of neglecting them. They hold the key to the past; they are the past. They are therefore afforded a particular dignity and they are respected. But in industrialised countries, old people have lost their dignity and their place in society. They are no longer capable of earning money, and so they are seen as a burden.

In our rich societies, a wall stands between the strong and the weak. People in need are seen first and foremost as an economic burden. They are taken into the care of professionals, social workers, teachers; as a result, the rest of society no longer considers itself either individually or collectively responsible for them. People no longer consider them part of their family or community. They hand over all their responsibilities to the state. Of course, the state relies on private associations and encourages charities. But nevertheless the feeling of solidarity has been lost. And because looking after the weaker members of society is expensive, there comes a time of economic crisis when the system ceases to function. The weak people become an intolerable burden, so it becomes necessary to get rid of them. They are a drain on resources preventing other people from carrying out more interesting, important work.

The wall of fear surrounding death

My sister Thérèse has spent twenty-five years working as a doctor in palliative care at St Christopher's Hospice in London. Through her, I have learned about the tragedy of many people dying in hospitals, the tragedy which inspired Cecily Saunders to create St Christopher's Hospice. When someone who is seriously ill enters a terminal phase, there comes a point when there is no longer anything that can medically be done for them, the vital organs are irremediably weakened. The cancer has spread, and nothing can stop its growth. Most hospital doctors then feel helpless; they often prescribe large doses of morphine which take away the pain but which leave the sick person pretty well unconscious. Faced with situations like this, Cecily Saunders felt inspired to do something. She believed that the end of somebody's life was a moment of great importance, and that what was necessary was to find the means of controlling pain and helping dying people to be comfortable, so that they could die in as little pain as possible, whilst remaining fully conscious. She also thought that it was necessary to support their family and friends, so that they could talk to the dying person honestly and without hiding behind illusions and false hopes. Most people are scared of death and do not like to talk about it. They pretend it will not happen.

The refusal to accept death is particularly strong in America, where corpses are hurriedly carried off to funeral parlours where they are made to look as attractive as possible. The family of the person who has died is no longer allowed to keep the body at home. Fortunately, in other countries this does not happen; one is still allowed to watch and pray by the body for several days, to speak about the person who has died and allow the reality of the death to sink in.

In poorer countries, death is part of daily life; it is impossible to pretend it will not happen. Being born and dying are part of being human, however much people in more sophisticated societies try to shy away from death. They tend to talk about it as if it was an accident or an illness for which we have yet to find the remedy, as if death were a mistake and should not really exist. They build a wall between death and life. Freud said that the person who wants to live fully must make death a part of his, or her, life. We cannot really live fully if, either consciously or unconsciously, we are paralysed by a terror of death.

The walls surrounding prisons

During the seventies, I was often invited to talk to men, and sometimes women, who were serving sentences in Canadian prisons. In one prison in western Canada, I was even allowed to lead prisoners in a time of quiet reflection and prayer. I stayed in the prison for several days and had my own cell. At night, as I looked at the moon and the stars through the barred window, I felt a deep solidarity with all the men and women in prisons around the world. During this time, I was invited to spend an evening with Club 21, the club for men convicted of murder who were serving prison sentences of twenty-one years or more. A great number of them talked to me about what had happened to them. I became aware that, had I been born into a different family and had a different education, and had I had the kinds of experiences that these men had had, I might well have done what they had done. They were now living in a world devoid of tenderness, a world of anger and violence, surrounded by a vast wall. On one side of the wall, the condemned; on the other the so-called 'just' who judge severely those in prison. In fact, many of them had effectively received their sentences as tiny children. They had been born into broken and violent families, and brought up surrounded by misery and unemployment. Many were Amerindians, the native people of Canada, who could no longer find a place in the Western society which was so foreign to their culture, and which had imposed itself on their land.

In another Canadian prison, I gave a talk about people we had welcomed to l'Arche, about the rejection they had suffered, and the broken self-images they had developed as a result. In talking about what they had experienced, I knew that I was also talking about what the prisoners had experienced. At the end of my talk, a man stood up and screamed at me: 'You have had an easy life. You know nothing about our lives. When I was four, I watched my mother being raped in front of me. When I was seven, my father sold me into homosexual prostitution so that he could have money for drink. When I was thirteen, the men in blue [the police] came to get me.' He ended up by shouting: 'If another man comes to this prison to talk to us about love, I'll kick his bloody head in.'

I am always amazed by the similarities between people in prison and people with mental handicaps. Both are placed in institutions, behind walls and doors locked to prevent their moving about freely. Most have never known a happy, warm, secure family life. All the time, they carry around with them the stigma of being who and what they are. This leads to the development of deep wounds in their hearts, and these in turn lead some to become aggressive and violent, others depressive and closed in on themselves, filled with violence which they direct against themselves.

The walls around refugee camps

Some time ago I visited Slovenia, the little country in the former Yugoslavia with a population of about two million. It became independent in 1992 and there is a great homogeneity amongst its citizens: they share the same religion, culture and language. Their government had welcomed tens of thousands of refugees from Bosnia and I was able to visit one of the refugee camps.

The camp was a fenced-off area for a few hundred people, most of them Muslim. They had nothing to do all day but sit around and talk. There was a school for the small children, but nothing for the teenagers. They had sunk into complete apathy. The food brought to them from the town was already prepared and cooked. One of the families asked me into their 'home', a room in a wooden shack. I asked them if they had hope. 'No,' they answered, 'our village has been totally destroyed. We will never go back; we have lost everything.' I was struck by the indifference of the local population towards these refugees. There were no physical walls between the camp and them, but the psychological wall was enormous. It was as if the people living near the refugee camp just did not want to allow themselves to admit its existence. If they had begun to make friends with the refugees, to listen to them talking about what had happened to them and to look at the conditions in which they were living, they would have felt forced to act. They would have had to find work for them, or at least to do something to make their lives more bearable. This would have demanded both time and money, so it seemed better just to ignore them. 'And anyway,' one of them said to me, 'as they are Muslims, they could never really become integrated in our society.' Some situations are just too complicated. If we try to help just a little bit, we find ourselves completely overwhelmed by the needs of people, so it seems necessary to leave them in their misery. In every country, there are situations similar to the one I saw in that refugee camp in Slovenia.

The walls between people, races and nations

In 1982, a l'Arche community was created among the Palestinians in the occupied territories. We had found a little house belonging to a couple called Ali and Fatma, not too far from the mosque at Bethany. There we welcomed first Rula, then Ghadir, then others with mental handicaps. During one of my visits to this community, I became aware of the brutality of the conflict between Israelis and Palestinians, and of the thick and apparently impenetrable wall of hatred and fear that had grown up between the two peoples. When I visited a Jewish friend in Jerusalem, he asked me if I was not frightened to live among the Palestinians. He had a completely warped idea of what these people were like. For him, every Palestinian was a dangerous beast, a terrorist ready to murder everyone. For some, a terrorist is a criminal; for others he is a freedom fighter. If one day freedom fighters take power and find that they are legal, others fight them and themselves become terrorists and criminals.

In the evening, from the roof of Ali's house, we could see the Israeli soldiers on the roofs of the neighbouring houses scanning their surroundings suspiciously. They created an atmosphere of fear. They were young soliders and they too were afraid. Many of our young Palestinian neighbours were in prison; some did not even know what for. The living conditions in the prison were terrible. There was an immense wall between these two peoples. Now, a peace process has begun. Perhaps one day they will be able to live together.

In 1991 I went to Auschwitz to accompany some young men and women who had invited me to join them there. We walked across Camp 2, which was specially designed for the extermination of the Jews. The barracks where Jewish men and women, reduced to skeletons, had waited to be taken to the gas chambers were still there. Their bodies had then been burned in the crematorium, and their ashes scattered on the grass. Hundreds of thousands of men and women had been killed in this camp, martyrs to their race. The horror of it is that the Nazis proclaimed this work of mass murder to be a mission of liberation for humanity. My companions and I walked in silence asking God to take from our hearts our prejudices and our capacity to hurt others, especially those different from ourselves or weaker. Human beings can so easily become caught up in hatred and fear and falsehood, refusing to see and accept our common humanity.

In Bosnia a fire of hatred has spread between the Serbs, the Croats and the Muslims. There, where men and women of different races and religions lived together more or less peaceably, a civil war of desperate cruelty raged. Men have behaved like savage beasts, maddened by hatred, anguish and a thirst for vengeance. In their lust for blood, they have even massacred innocents.

I remain horrified by the massacres in Rwanda. Some months before they began, I visited that country to spend some time with the Faith and Light communities there. Today, many of my Rwandan friends are dead, victims of human passion and prejudice. Murdering other people because they are different from us is like murdering the shadow side that we each carry within ourselves.

Among the most terrible walls that our age has known is the Iron Curtain, a wall that completely closed off all the countries under the power of the former Soviet Union from the rest of the world. Behind the Iron Curtain, a vast network of police stopped people from communicating freely with one another, and a propoganda machine churned out lies, working to prove that Communism was the only system that brought people justice and happiness. Only things that supported the regime were seen as having value; anything not conforming to it was seen as evil. Truth eventually caused this wall to fall, but it stood for many years, imprisoning people in fear.

Jerusalem, city of God and of walls of hatred

It is painful to think about Jerusalem. It is a city full of people certain that they are right. The Jews know that they are Yahweh's chosen people. The Muslims know that they are blessed by Allah. The Christians know that they are chosen by Jesus, the saviour of the world. And it is even more complicated than this. Among the Jews, there are the Orthodox and those who are more liberal; among

14

the Muslims, there are Shiites, Sunni and other groups descended from the Prophet; among the Christians, there are Lutherans, Anglicans, Catholics, Orthodox, Baptists, Methodists, Pentecostalists . . . ! Each group is certain that it has the truth of Jesus, the unique revelation from God. So are there a number of Gods? Or is God divided? Jerusalem, the city of God, the city of love, has become a city of division and hatred. The walls of Jerusalem are beautiful but terrible. It is hardly surprising that many people nowadays tend to reject religion altogether, seeing it as a source of hatred and war and contempt for others. But even those who have no religion, or who rail against religion, are sometimes sure that, in thinking that religion is the root of all the conflict in the world, they are the only ones who are really enlightened.

Each church proclaims its truth and knows that it is right. Every Christian church claims that Jesus is Lord, but sometimes it seems that there must be as many Jesuses as churches! I remember once being in the tiny chapel under the Basilica of the Nativity in Bethlehem. An Orthodox priest was celebrating the liturgy. I was praying among the Orthodox pilgrims. There came a moment at which a plate with blessed bread was passed around (it was not Holy Communion). Somebody offered it to me, but another shouted: 'No! Not him. He's a Catholic.' I felt waves of tension. A little later, a woman approached me discreetly and, with great kindness, shared her bread with me. Her gentle kindness touched me. How deeply some Protestants have suffered through being refused, without explanation, the Holy Communion that is at the heart of Catholic Mass.

There are also divisions within every church and every religion. There are always people who want at all costs to safeguard their dogmas, traditions and rites, their religious identity and moral teachings. Then there are those who are more open, more tolerant, who see that it is important to have contact and communication with people as they are, who are not necessarily of the same religion, and who see that these people have value and real beauty. For the former, religion is like a fortress: the good people are inside, the bad outside; authority is sovereign. For the latter, religion is more like a well from which the whole of humanity is called to receive life; but their openness and willingness to listen to others can also lead to a gradual decay of their faith. These two tendencies, which appear irreconcilable, reveal not only the kind of spiritual and theological formation people have had but also their different psychological make-up. There are those whose personalities are rigid, fixed, conservative, rather insecure; and there are others who are more open, who like taking risks, who do not see things in black-and-white terms, and who are sometimes suspicious of authority. People at each of these extremes feel that they are in the right, and see the others as a threat; they believe themselves to be the élite. Throughout history, the struggles between these extremes have led to catastrophes: mutual condemnations, excommunications, imprisonments and burnings at the stake. A minister of the Pentecostal Church of Russia once said to me: 'When we were in prison [Christians of different denominations], we were united. But now we are free, we no longer talk to each other. New walls stand between us. We learned how to live together in prison, but now we don't know how to cope with freedom.'

In 1974, I took part in an ecumenical retreat in Belfast in Northern Ireland. Thirty Catholics and thirty Protestants participated. None of the Catholics had ever spoken to a Protestant before, and vice versa. Between the two religions of Northern Ireland, there was, and still is, a vast wall of prejudice, misunderstanding and ignorance. Each group lived in its own area of the town, avoiding any contact or dialogue with the other. Each had its own set of convictions, and its own ways of slanting information and justifying itself. Each was convinced that the people on the other side were bad and dangerous, that nothing good could possibly come from them. There was no point in discussing things with them, because 'they would just try to catch us out'. Fear, fear whipped up through false information and lies, manipulated by hatred and by a little group thirsty for power, separates people and groups, and creates walls of prejudice. Atrocities provoke further atrocities; vengeance calls for further vengeance and so hatred escalates.

The walls between rich and poor

One day I was in the Metro in Paris. A man came into the compartment I was sitting in and began to shout: 'Give me money! I need money! If you don't give me some money, I'm going to do something stupid.' I had my back to him; I watched the passengers facing me bury themselves deeper into their newspapers and books. They did not want to hear this man's cry. They were afraid of him, and pretended that they could neither see nor hear him. Confronted with a beggar or a poor man's cry, we all feel a certain awkwardness. We justify paying no attention to them by telling ourselves: 'It's better not to give them money. They will only spend it on drink or drugs.' It was surely this same fear that was in the hearts of the priest and the Levite in Jesus's parable of the Good Samaritan (Luke 10:29). A man had been attacked and beaten up by bandits somewhere between Jerusalem and Jericho. They left him half dead. First a priest and then a Levite passed by. They saw him, but carried on walking. They were afraid to stop. Then a Samaritan passed by. He stopped and helped the man. In the time of Christ, the Samaritans were rejected as schismatic by the orthodox Jews.

We are all afraid of the cry of the poor, afraid when we see a man lying, beaten up, on the ground. If we stop to help a person like this, we are bound to lose something – time, money, possibly more. Someone might accuse us of having been the one who beat the person up. So we justify our inaction saying, 'I haven't got time, and what's more I can't give money to everybody, and in any case these people get what they deserve.' We do not want to get our hands dirty.

Perhaps at a deeper level we have a vague idea that what the poor man really wants is solidarity, friendship and communion. But we ourselves are poor in our ability to love and in our readiness to change. So a wall has grown up between those who are well integrated in society, and those who have been pushed aside.

Jesus describes this situation in another parable (Luke 16:19): the parable of Lazarus and the rich man. Lazarus, a starving beggar whose legs were covered in sores, would have loved to have eaten the scraps which fell from the rich man's table. Lazarus could see the rich man feasting at home with his friends; his dogs were eating the scraps. One day, Lazarus died. He was taken up into the bosom of Abraham, a place of peace and happiness. Then the rich man died and went to a place of torment. From there, he cried to Abraham: 'Father Abraham, send Lazarus to put a drop of cold water on my lips, for I am dying of thirst.' And Abraham replied: 'That is impossible, because there is an impassable gulf between you and him.' The gulf that existed between Lazarus and the rich man while they were alive – but which was psychological rather than physical – continues to exist after death. The rich man did not notice Lazarus when he was a beggar; he could not see him as a human being, a brother with whom he shared a common humanity.

The Hindu religion takes a fatalistic view of society. A person is born into a caste, and cannot move out of it; each person has his or her place in the human hierarchy. This can sometimes be a way of justifying injustice and poverty. The same kind of idea is found in Greek philosophy; a wall stands between masters and slaves. Some say this is the natural order, and it must not be disturbed or we risk creating disorder.

Once we accept the idea that the life of every human being is sacred and precious, that each person has rights and responsibilities, this wall that separates people and causes oppression becomes intolerable. This is why in certain Latin American and Asian countries, the cry of peasants without land or rights is raised against the few families who possess most of the land. In North America and Australia, native people cry out their anger against those who have taken their land, who have oppressed them and treated them as inferior.

On the shores of Lake Michigan, on which Chicago is situated, there is the Gold Coast. This is an area of super-luxury buildings, where the richest people live. Only a few roads away from there are the slums where the black people live. The houses are dilapidated and squalid; it is a world of deprivation and violence. Between the rich area and the black ghetto there is a thick, psychological wall. Fear prevents the people in the two areas from communicating with one another. The rich people have the power and the police, they are frightened of the world of poverty and perhaps they feel guilty about their wealth. Meanwhile, the poor are living in a world of depression and anger. The rich seem to be blessed by God, while the poor seem damned, abandoned to violence, misery and death.

In our age, in every country, unemployment is increasing. Unemployed men and women lose confidence in themselves, in their capacity to be human. They are bored to death. They move often from failure to failure, from rejection to rejection. They are ashamed to face their children. They live behind a wall of sadness.

The Psalmist tells us that God hears the cry of the poor. We human beings are afraid of this cry; it undermines our comfort, our security and our well-being. We avoid the poor; we do not want to look at them. An official in an African country once said to me when I tried to explain to him what l'Arche was about, 'It's a good thing you've come here. Somebody really needs to take the mad people off our streets.' Poor people embarrass and upset us. They arouse conflicting feelings of pity, anger, inner discomfort and perhaps a kind of more or less recognised guilt. They reveal our selfishness, our human poverty, our refusal to stand by one another. It is not surprising that the rich defend themselves and try to hide poor people behind the walls of slum areas.

The wall of competition: the need to be the best

At school, I was encouraged to be the best, the best academically and the best at sport. In the navy, I had to strive to excel, to impress my superiors, to succeed, to win admiration and promotion which brought privileges and a higher salary.

There are, of course, good things about competition: the desire to come first encourages people to make an effort, to push themselves to the limit. This helps combat laziness and carelessness. Competition awakens energies; it helps people to develop their potential, and in so doing to develop the potential of society and of humanity. But while some people win, the majority lose. A culture thus develops in which those who do not succeed are rejected. Power, competence and excellence then become the only values. Unsuccessful people are seen as having no value and are pushed aside. They develop broken images of themselves, and lose confidence in themselves; they feel worthless.

Aristotle says that when a person does not feel loved, he or she seeks to be admired. To be neither loved nor admired is like death. Human beings need the attention of others who appreciate, love, admire and affirm them. If they do not get this, or if the people around them despise them, reject them, fear them, or treat them as if they do not exist, then emptiness, anguish and depression engulf them. People will do anything to find someone who will affirm them and make them feel valued.

A priest friend of mine, a prison chaplain, once told me about a prisoner who had asked him, 'Do you like saying Mass? Do you do it well? Do you like preaching? Do you preach well?' A bit embarrassed, my friend answered 'yes' to all these questions. The prisoner then said, 'Well, I'm the best car thief in Cleveland, and I like that!' If a person does not feel loved and admired for his good qualities, he will seek to be admired for his destructive powers, even for his ability to hate. The need to be the strongest and best in a particular field is so powerful in the human heart. It seems to be a question of life and death.

There is the desire to win as an individual. There is also the desire that the group to which we belong should win. If you want proof of this, you have only to look at the passion with which certain people watch rugby and football matches on television. They shout, they clap, they cry; they live a thousand emotions while they watch their team throwing themselves at this wretched piece of leather filled with air, as their team moves towards victory or defeat.

There can sometimes be real beauty in sport, real excellence. Very often, however, people are not so interested in the beauty or the excellence as in being identified with the winning team.

One day, I was walking with Nadine in Tegucigalpa in Honduras. Suddenly, everyone on the street seemed to go mad. They jumped in the air, howling with joy, throwing their arms round one another. We had no idea what was going on. Then Nadine remembered that Honduras was playing football against Guatemala. All these people jumping about were listening to the match on their walkmans.

The more we lack personal identity and success, or feel a failure, the more we feel the need to identify ourselves with a group, a social class, a country, a race or a religion which is thriving. The love of a nation, a race or a religion can become tremendously powerful in arousing the energies of individuals and getting them to engage in a struggle, in inspiring them to use all their strength so that their side wins and gets the better of any rivals.

The need to win and succeed can also be linked to the desire to have a role which brings privileges, to exercise power, to impose our will on others. Some people exert their power solely in order to demonstrate their superiority. In order to feel alive, they need their power to be obvious. They demonstrate it by shouting, by refusing others permission or by giving permission only when it is going to make them popular. They work not for the good and enlightenment and growth of others, but because of their own needs and for their own glory. This is one of the dangers that people who work with those weaker than themselves have to look out for – the need to feel superior, to impose their own will, vision, choices and superior strength on others.

The need to win is often so strong that small disagreements can blow up into bitter and futile quarrels. What fierce arguments we are prepared to enter into, just in order to prove that we are right! How many arguments between husbands and wives are just attempts to prove that 'I am right and you are wrong'! People who feel they are no good quickly think they are at fault; then they begin to feel empty, even dead inside. Sometimes, people in this position are ready to cheat, to lie, to use all kinds of unjust and illegal methods in order to prove that they exist, to exercise power and influence and to be recognised and held in high esteem.

This kind of cheating and lying in order to gain and hang on to power is particularly obvious in the world of politics. Politics can very quickly degenerate into battles and competitions between factions and candidates whose chief aim is to get power for themselves. They are sometimes ready to deceive everybody simply in order to project the kind of image of themselves that will secure them power. This is why people in positions of power so often become inaccessible. They hide behind secretaries and personal assistants who protect them from the public. Sometimes they do this so as to hide their incompetence, their human poverty, the fact that they are incapable of listening, or of using their power to serve others.

In some, the thirst for power seems limitless. They want constantly to increase their empire and their zone of influence. Dictators and mafia chiefs are the most obvious examples of this frantic desire to govern others, to be like God and be subject to nobody. Yet a little dictator is hidden inside each one of us. We all tend to want to exert power and control others. It may only be over a small group – the people who work for us, our families and friends – but the dictator is there nonetheless, ready to burst forth in order to rule, control, be superior.

A huge wall separates those who have been successful

from those who have known failure, like the rich man from Lazarus. On one side of the wall is success, power and what appears to be life; on the other, poverty and death. And people tend to fight for life and success at any price, even when it means turning their backs on truth, justice and compassion. People are ready to destroy their competitors, to prove that they are no good, and sometimes to encourage suspicious rumours about their morals and their private lives, to humiliate them just in order to gain power for themselves. But the number of people on the poor side of the wall never ceases to swell, and at some point the poor come together. Their anger in the face of injustice becomes so great that one day it erupts in violence. Those who have been oppressed seize power. They then proceed to oppress those who have oppressed them, until the time comes when these, in turn, revolt. And so, throughout the history of humanity, violence erupts again and again.

In this universe, we have the high and the low, the sun and the mud, the beautiful and the hideous. Very quickly, we human beings divide ourselves into groups that clearly define pure and impure, good and bad, competent and incompetent, the virtuous and the sinners. Walls separate these groups. Children from good families are forbidden to play with children from bad families. Those who consider themselves pure feel superior and proud. Those who are supposedly impure – alcoholics, drug addicts, people whose sexuality is disturbed – feel guilty, confused, depressed, despairing. They have broken self-images.

Today, AIDS is the illness of shame. The brother of an assistant at l'Arche died of AIDS on Good Friday, at about three o'clock in the afternoon. His father had refused to see him when he knew he had AIDS. Father and son were separated by a wall of shame.

Perhaps we all know this little tale. The head of a company

shouts unfairly at one of his employees. The employee feels bruised and wounded, but he does not dare answer back. He goes home seething with rage. Supper is not ready, so he screams at his wife, taking out all his anguish and suppressed anger on her. She does not dare answer back. Instead, when she sees her son about to take something from the fridge, she shouts at him. He says nothing; he is frightened of being smacked, so he goes out into the road and kicks a dog. The dog chases a cat, who runs and kills a mouse. This is the way that aggression is passed on from person to person, from group to group, from generation to generation. It provokes fear, which in turn provokes the desire to hurt and to destroy. And there is always the person at the end of the line who cannot reply, who receives the violence of others, and remains silent, deeply wounded. Is this not, in some way, the situation of people with mental handicaps, or of aborted children? They receive the violence of the world but they cannot respond – they are at the end of the line.

The fear of people different from ourselves

Nearly every one of us belongs to a group of people similar to ourselves, sharing our beliefs and values. Each group, whether national, racial, political, religious or anti-religious, thinks that it is the best and knows what is true. The other groups are seen as inferior, as wrong in some way. A wall separates us from them. It is easy to judge others, but so difficult to look critically at ourselves and the group to which we belong. The person who is different, the stranger, makes us feel uneasy. The way others live, the things they believe, their views about the truth, their clothes, traditions, languages and religious values are so different that we find it difficult to listen to them, to respect them and above all to integrate them into our own convictions and way of looking at life. The convictions of those who are different from us make us question our own convictions. They disturb us and sow seeds of doubt. And the more we believe that we are superior and the élite of the world, the more impossible it is for us to see ourselves as we really are. So the stranger and those who are different will make us feel even more uneasy. We do not really want to listen to them with open hearts. If we listen to them at all, it is with suspicion and fear; we interpret their words according to our prejudices.

Fear born of difference can exist between men and women, and between generations. Parents think they know what is good for their children. Teenagers, meanwhile, judge their parents. They do not want to be told what to do. They want to be independent. In this way walls build up between people and groups.

Protective walls

Walls are not just negative things, separating and dividing human beings. They also protect life and enable it to grow. The mother's womb protects the tiny, newly conceived child. The walls of a house secure the privacy and life of a family; they provide security. All of us, in order to live and become fully ourselves, need a private space, a place of solitude and protection. We particularly need it in times of weakness, exhaustion or illness. Generally speaking, human beings tend to protect themselves, often unconsciously, against any situation which threatens their physical or psychological well-being. We are overcome with panic if anyone intrudes on our private space, or if a stranger tries to get too close to us physically, emotionally or spiritually. Walls protect life. There are hostile and destructive forces at work in our world and our society and we need to be on our guard.

Equally, in order to live fully as human beings, we need to have a definite identity, to belong to a group which shares our values and gives us some security. Without this identity, who are we? We are swallowed up in chaos, or in trying to be what others want us to be. We no longer exist. Sometimes it is necessary for people to discover and deepen their identity by hiding behind walls. Once they know who they are, they can begin to open themselves to others.

If walls offer individuals protection against outside violation or intrusion, they also protect these same individuals from damaging others through their own disordered desires and instincts. They help people to contain their violence, their sexual desires and their selfish needs. People who have no internal barriers can erupt too quickly into violence. They can harm others and themselves. This is why psychiatric hospitals and prisons, so long as they are run in a way that is humane and genuinely therapeutic, can be necessary to help certain people whose inner balance is too fragile. These people can then be helped to recover a sense of who they are, with their own dignity, and refind the right inner protective walls.

We need walls to protect ourselves and to allow our lives to deepen and grow, but the danger comes when they become walls of fear and intolerance. Our challenge as human beings is to discern when it is necessary to maintain walls in order to protect life, and when we can let them come down so that we can allow people who are different to get close to us, so that they can make their home in us and we in them, and so that we can grow towards mutual enrichment and give life to others. How can we achieve this? How can we discover the common humanity that is deeper than all our differences? This is the subject of this book.

I would like to begin this book by explaining how we human beings are made for communion and peace, and how our inner walls begin to form. Exterior walls are only the extension of our own inner walls. These walls, and even the walls of prejudice and hatred, are not static and immovable; they are walls of fear but also of life. And life is always growing and evolving. Fear can disappear. The wall which at one moment shelters and protects can become a prison wall which keeps out life. And this prison wall can gradually disappear through a rebirth of trust.

One of the walls I am most struck by is that around the hearts and spirits of people whom we call 'psychotic'. It seems very thick. It is built to protect these people from the unbearable anguish which they often suffer in their relationships with others. But people suffering from psychotic illness are often, in the deepest parts of themselves, incredibly sensitive. If these people are in the right sort of environment and if they find the support that they need (sometimes with the help of the right medication), these walls begin to crumble. Communication can be restored.

The Berlin Wall fell without anyone firing a single shot. It collapsed in ruins like other walls have done, before the forces of life and liberty. The wall of apartheid fell beneath the power of thousands of men and women like Mandela and de Klerk who were courageous in their belief in human liberty and universal communion. Similarly, a tenuous peace process is underway between Israel and the Palestinians; the walls of fear and hatred are beginning to weaken.

In one of the villages where we have a l'Arche community, there was a very difficult, unpleasant man. He seemed to hate people with mental handicaps, and to hate the l'Arche community. He shouted at us and made threats. He terrified people by charging at them in his tractor. Then one day

Nicholas, a man with a mental handicap, went to see him to ask him whether he would look after his rabbit during the holidays. He said he would. A bond was formed. Gradually, the man changed and now, from time to time, he comes to eat with the community. His threats have given way to gestures of friendship and welcome. The walls of hatred and fear have disappeared and trust is beginning to flow.

II

COMMUNION
AND WOUNDEDNESS

1 The thirst for communion

Since I was a child, there have been three very distinct stages in my life. When I was thirteen, I joined the navy and spent eight years in a world where weakness was something to be shunned at all costs. We were required to be efficient and quick and to climb up the ladder of success. I left this world, and another world opened up to me – the world of thought. For many years, I studied philosophy. I wrote a doctoral thesis on Aristotelian ethics and I embarked on a teaching career. Once again, I found myself in a world where weakness, ignorance and incompetence were things to be shunned – efficiency was everything. Then, during a third phase, I discovered people who were weak, people with mental handicaps. I was moved by the vast world of poverty, weakness and fragility that I encountered in hospitals, institutions and asylums for people with mental handicaps. I moved from the world of theories and ideas about human beings in order to discover what it really meant to be human, to be a man or a woman.

I was touched by these men with mental handicaps, by their sadness and by their cry to be respected, valued and loved. In welcoming Raphael and Philippe, I discovered something about communion. Raphael and Philippe did not want to live with a retired naval officer who ordered everybody about and thought himself superior.

Nor did they want to live with an ex-professor of philosophy who thought he knew a lot. They wanted to live with a friend. And what is a friend if not someone who does not judge me, who does not abandon me when he discovers my weaknesses, limitations, wounds, shortcomings, everything that is broken within me? A friend is someone who sees my true beauty and potential, and who wants to help me to develop them. A friend is happy to be with me. He feels joy in being with me.

In living with Raphael and Philippe, I began to discover the thirst for communion that was in them and is in every human being. What mattered to Raphael and Philippe was not the methods I used to teach them to be more independent and to work, but my attitude to them. They cared most about the way I listened to them, understood them and their needs, and treated them with respect and love; the way I responded to their requests and was able to be joyful, celebrate and laugh with them. It was through these things that they were able, little by little, to discover their own beauty, that their lives had meaning and worth. For many years, their parents and the society in which they lived had pitied them, and let them know that they were a disappointment to all, that they had no value as human beings, that they were, humanly speaking, a failure. As I lived with them, and found my joy in them, they were able to discover their uniqueness, their fundamental beauty, and so regain their self-confidence. They did not have to do any more than simply be themselves in order to be loved. This was a radical departure, a kind of rebirth for them; and for me too, because through my cultural background and education I was a man of competition, not of communion. Raphael and Philippe brought me on a road of conversion. Like all conversions, it is not yet complete.

Communion, generosity and collaboration

I began to discover that communion is very different from generosity. Generosity consists in doing good to others, in giving our time or money, in devoting ourselves to others and to their good. Generous people are in a strong position; they have talents, power and wealth; they do good things for others but do not receive from them. They are not vulnerable to love. Similarly, communion is different to education, where one person teaches others and remains superior to them; one has power, the others do not.

When we enter into communion with somebody, we become vulnerable and open ourselves to each other. There is a reciprocity, which communicates itself through the eyes and through touch. There is a sort of to-and-fro of love, a mutual understanding and respect which can lead people to share, laugh and celebrate together, or, in times of sorrow, to weep together. They speak heart to heart. Communion is founded on mutual trust in which a person gives to and receives from another that which is deepest and most silent in their being.

I discovered equally that communion is very different from collaboration or co-operation. When people collaborate, they work together towards the same end, in sports, in the navy or in a commercial venture, for example. They are brought together by a common goal, but there is not necessarily communion between them. They are not personally vulnerable one to another. When there is communion between people, they sometimes work together, but what matters to them is not that they succeed in achieving some target, but simply that they are together, that they find their joy in one another and care for one another. Raphael and Philippe really led me into this world of communion. When I was in the navy, I did not seek to enter into communion with the men under my command. I gave them orders. I was superior to them. If they failed in some way or found themselves in difficulties, I had either to try to resolve their problems or to reprimand them. When I was a teacher, I had to tell the students what they needed to do or learn, I had to correct their work, to inspire them intellectually. With Raphael and Philippe, what was needed was to create a warm atmosphere where we could be bonded together in love and in mutual commitment, and where we could live in communion with one another as if we were a family.

Communion first manifests itself in the love of a mother or father for their child. The mother rejoices when her little girl smiles, and the child rejoices in the smile of her mother. They open themselves to one another. They are awakening and warming each other's hearts. It is impossible to say whether the mother is giving more to her little girl or the girl to her mother. This communion is transmitted through play, smiles and how we touch or look at each other, through times when the child is being fed and bathed and cared for. The mother laughs and plays and cuddles her child, and the child responds by smiling and laughing, and becoming completely relaxed. Certainly, the child is dependent on the mother. She needs the security that her parents give. It is obvious that she cannot be generous because she has nothing of her own to give. But she can give her joy, her smiles, and most of all her trust. Trust is a beautiful form of love, where we give our hearts and minds.

Between mother and child there is a to-and-fro of love. In the way that they touch and look at their child, the mother or father is saying, 'You are beautiful, you are lovable, you are precious, you matter to us.' And the child is saying the same to them. When she looks at them, and when she laughs, the child is revealing their beauty to them. They respond to the love and trust of the child. Obviously, for the child this communion is instinctive. It does not flow from a choice or from a rational understanding or consciousness. It flows from a deep need of love; it flows as a response to love. Love calls forth love.

However fragile this communion is, it is nevertheless of profound importance; it is fundamental to the life of every human being. It is the foundation from which each person is able gradually to open up to others, to enter into communion with them and with the universe, to see them as friends who can be trusted, and not as enemies. A little girl who has not lived this communion cannot have confidence; she will live in fear and create systems of defence and aggression in order to protect herself. The world will become, or at least seem to her, a hostile place.

Eric

One of the people who taught me most about what communion really is was a man called Eric. We first met him in a psychiatric hospital when he was sixteen years old. He was blind and deaf, and he could not walk, talk, or feed himself. He had a severe mental handicap. His mother, though a good woman, was not able to cope with her child's suffering. She felt unable to help him, and she put him into a general hospital when he was four. He was later transferred to the children's ward in a psychiatric hospital. Small and weak, he could not understand why his mother was no longer with him, why all of a sudden he was being handled, sometimes roughly, by all sorts of different people. He was lost and confused. The things which had become familiar to him, and which he had come to rely on, had vanished. He felt alone in a hostile world.

When I met him, Eric had already spent twelve years in the psychiatric hospital. He had severe emotional disorders. His heart was like an enormous void full of fear and anguish. When I came close to him, he took my hands or my feet and then began to cling to me and howl with the whole of his being, crying out to be touched and loved. His cry was so aggressive, so total, that it was unbearable to listen to it. It was as if I would be devoured unless I freed myself from his grasp. It was clear that at the hospital he was regarded as an impossible child, far too demanding. There was no joy in being with him. He was deeply distressed and restless, and the nurses found it impossible to deal with him. So his anguish and his aggression increased, until they were unbearable for him and for those around him. He could not keep still, he was incontinent, he behaved roughly. Sometimes he let out terrible cries. It was clear that, inside himself, he had formed a terribly broken self-image.

Many children with severe handicaps live as Eric lived. People do not know how to deal with them. Their parents cannot always give them the love and communion, the tenderness and the care which they need. A little boy cannot live except through communion, through the looks and hands and tenderness of his mother. All alone, he is in danger. He cannot take care of himself, he is too small, vulnerable, defenceless and helpless. If he feels that he is unloved, unwanted, that there is no place for him, he falls into terrible anguish. He lives through traumas of fear, because if he is not loved and protected, then he is really in danger of death. This is the tragedy of the abandoned child. Sensing himself alone, rejected, he begins to believe that he has been abandoned because he is bad. He then feels guilty about existing. He is a nuisance to everyone.

He has hurt his family. He enters then into a vicious circle of inner suffering. He feels that no one wants him, and so he becomes more anguished, depressive and aggressive. He closes in on himself more and more, so people become more and more afraid of him. He is forced to defend himself as best he can in a hostile world.

When we welcome people like Eric to l'Arche, the one thing that we need to show them is that we are happy that they exist, that we love them and accept them just as they are. But how do we show this to someone like Eric who can neither see nor hear? It is impossible to say it in words, or to demonstrate it through actions. It can only be expressed through touch. After I ceased to be director of l'Arche in 1980, I had the privilege of spending a year with Eric in one of our houses in Trosly which we call 'La Forestière'. There I discovered that one of the special moments for building communion was bath time. Eric's tiny body relaxed in the warm water, and he obviously enjoyed it. He was so happy to be held and washed. The only language he could understand was that of tenderness transmitted through our hands – a language of gentleness and security, but also a language which, through my touch, revealed to him that he was lovable and that I was happy in his presence. And in touching him, I received from him the trust and tenderness that he wanted to show me.

The body is the fundamental instrument of communion. Communion demands a certain quality of listening, which is revealed through our attentiveness. With our bodies, with the way we look and listen, we can reveal to somebody their importance and uniqueness. When we listen to a little boy with interest, he discovers that he has something to say, and very often he wants to say it there and then. If, on the other hand, we talk all the time and are endlessly telling him what he should be doing or how he should be developing, then he may have difficulty in finding confidence in himself and he will probably refuse to speak.

Communication: the language of love

At l'Arche, I have learned a lot about language. In the navy, and when I was studying, language was simply a means of telling people what to do, of exchanging information and of discussing things. Often, by showing off our knowledge, we demonstrated our superiority. We entered into discussions in order to prove something, we gave orders and we taught. There was also the language of relaxation: we told stories, joked, fooled around so as to become the centre of attention. The language of friendship is more personal. At l'Arche, I discovered the language of love, playfulness and celebration. We use words in order to express our joy in one another, to give something of ourselves to others, to show others that we love them and to live communion. The language is no longer one of competition; it is one of celebration, revelation, intimate exchanges through smiling and laughter. Of course, with people who have mental handicaps, this language is often one of gesture and expression; we have to learn to interpret it. We have also to talk to them about what is going on and to explain that violent and antisocial behaviour has its limits. We have to demand that they make efforts in certain areas. We have to teach them to work. But first and foremost, language is used to build communion, and the language of communion is simple.

In building communion, the most important language is non-verbal, the language of the body – gestures, tone of voice, the look in our eyes. Through these we can express love, understanding, trust and interest in another or, equally, lack of interest, contempt, rejection. For those who have difficulty in speaking, the body becomes the main means of expression. Cries, violence, self-destructive acts, like gestures of tenderness, are all means of communication, they all carry messages.

A mother always interprets the cries of her child: 'My baby is hungry,' she will tell you; 'He is teething, he is sick; he needs to be loved, cuddled; he is angry . . .' In the same way at l'Arche we learn to read people's expressions, their eyes, their bodies, cries of anguish and gestures of tenderness. When a child or a woman who cannot express herself through words feels that she is understood, and that people are responding to her desires, a new confidence is born in her – the confidence that she is a person with a right to have and to express desires, a person who is understood, a belief that she is precious.

At the heart of l'Arche is celebration. The language of celebration uses the whole being, body and spirit. People like Eric have very broken images of themselves. For years and years they have been enveloped in sadness, in a language of disappointment and aggressiveness which has reinforced this negative self-image. They feel that they are good for nothing. But when they begin to feel that they are surrounded by joy, little by little they begin to discover that they are sources of joy, life and happiness. Their negative self-image gradually transforms itself into a positive one. When so-called 'normal' people become adolescents and adults, rational language frequently takes precedence over the language of communion. Communion can become a bit frightening because it implies vulnerability and the gift of self. Communion is not just a passing emotional experience in the child, but an experience which is written into each person's story. It is the gift of our deepest being and calls for continuity and fidelity. Words are necessary to articulate this. Sometimes, physical intimacy too quickly established can stifle or block the dialogue necessary to build up true communion between adults. With Raphael and Philippe, I needed to show my commitment to them. After three months in the little house, I asked them if they wanted to stay. They said that they did. I said that I too wanted them to stay. I said, 'You can stay here as long as you want. This is our home.'

Communion: the gift of freedom

Communion is not a fusion in which the frontiers between two people cease to exist and neither knows who is who. The mother knows that her little boy exists as an independent entity. She wants him to grow up and to become truly himself. The child very soon begins to show who he is and what he wants. There are, however, false communions which lead to unhealthy dependence. A mother might seek to manipulate her child emotionally in order to stop him becoming fully himself so that she can control him more easily. Possessive communion occurs when the mother uses the child in order to fulfil her own emotional needs. She seeks to hold on to her little boy, and to keep him for herself, so as to calm her own anguish. She cannot bear his cry for freedom, his refusal to obey. She cannot bear him to assert his independence. This is a caricature of communion, which often happens when a mother feels emotionally abandoned by her husband. She uses the child to fill her own emptiness.

True communion is a gift of the heart to help another to be as fully alive and free as possible. It is a pouring out of self for another. The mother rejoices because her child becomes himself; she shows him that his 'otherness' is the best thing about him. This is why the father is so important. Not only does he too live in communion with his child, but his love for his wife allows her to live this self-giving communion with her child. In fact, the communion between the parents and the child has its roots in the communion that exists between the father and mother.

True communion does not shut people off from others. On the contrary, it gives each person freedom and life. A mother is not closed in on her child; she does not shut herself away in her room with him. She shows him off, 'Look how beautiful he is!' And at the same time the child, in his own way, says, 'Look how beautiful she is!' True communion communicates to others this same joy, love, tenderness, unity and freedom lived between parents and their child.

Communion and touch

Communion implies a physical presence and is nourished by this presence. It is not just an intellectual or spiritual harmony. Communion is communicated through the body, the eyes, the smile, the tone of voice, through a handshake or a hug. Communion implies a warmth and openness which flow through the body. It implies some physical contact and touch. But 'touch' is an ambiguous term in English today, for it has taken on a sexual connotation and can be used as an euphemism for 'sexual abuse': 'Her father used to touch her when she was little.' Yet touch is at the heart of communion, and reveals presence, attentiveness and tenderness towards the other person. It reveals how we feel towards another. The way a mother holds her little boy, caresses him and bathes him, reveals her love for him and makes him feel safe. Handshakes can welcome us warmly or be a cold, brief formality. So touch and physical contact can be used to give life and security, but they can also be used for our own pleasure, to seduce or to have power over another person.

What is appropriate varies from situation to situation, and 'permissible' parts of the body or type of touch are defined differently according to each culture. Puberty brings enormous changes to the way we view touch, as our awareness of sexuality and what is erotic increases. This is one reason why sexual abuse of children has such traumatic effects, for it plunges them into the adult world of sex.

Perhaps the ambiguity of the word 'touch' reflects the ambiguity we feel about our bodies and our desires. If we are not at home in our bodies, not listening to them humbly, then they can be a source of fear. Our desires might be experienced as so strong, so overwhelming, that it is as if we have no control over them. Also, although we want and need to be touched in order to live communion, there can be a fear about the other's intentions. It can be easier to tolerate more affective physical contact from people with mental handicaps because with them there usually seems to be no ambiguity. Maybe that is why such people can have a healing effect on some people who are frightened of their own bodies.

Today there is a whole science of touch, 'haptonomia'. Through it people are trying to refind what should come spontaneously and naturally in relationships of love, trust and respect, but which has been deformed through a fear of our bodies or a desire to use people. Are we not all called to reveal to people through touch that we love them, that they are important and that we want them to be happy? Nurses and doctors are called to discover that touch is therapeutic, as are teachers and those working with people with special needs.

We can only touch with love and communicate safely if we are at home in our bodies. Our bodies bring us down to earth and into time; they remind us we are not immortal. If we are not at home in our bodies, or we deny that our natural desires exist, or we refuse to accept our bodies' needs or limitations, then our ability to be in communion with God or with others is impaired. Instead of 'touch' communicating life to another, it can be divorced from a desire for communion and can be used merely to fulfil our own needs. Respecting our bodies, seeing them as an integral part of our being, the temple of the heart through which the heart communicates life and tenderness, is all part of our journey towards wholeness.

Communion and time

Clearly, I could not live the communion I gradually discovered with Raphael and Philippe, or later with others like Eric, all the time. There were always things to be done: cooking, housework, organising the working day, and arranging outings. There were times when Raphael became angry, and moments when he suffered great anguish. I needed times to rest, be alone, pray or read. Raphael and Philippe needed times of solitude too. Life comes not only through communion and giving and receiving affection but also through growth, rest and nourishment in an atmosphere of peace and security. In a busy day, the times of communion are like moments of fullness. It is as if everything we do during the day finds its fulfilment as we share together quietly, look at each other tenderly, smile and laugh together. The silence and the feeling of stillness and rest can turn into prayer.

At La Forestière, after supper, I used to change Eric into his pyjamas. Then all of us – people with severe handicaps and assistants – would spend half or three quarters of an hour together in prayer in the living-room. I often sat with Eric on my knees. He rested, and I found that in his company I was able to rest too. I did not want to talk. I felt peaceful and silent. He was peaceful too. I felt contented, and so did he. It was a time of healing for me. I refound an inner unity and wholeness. A gentle smile seemed to flow into Eric's face. His body was no longer agitated. He was happy. It is like this when a little baby boy rests in the arms of his mother, and the mother in turn finds rest in her communion with him. These are moments of inner healing for both, for each through the other.

You can see this also between couples, or friends, or when two people have had a long talk together. There comes a moment of quiet and of peace. The two people are fully at ease, at home with each other. A silence descends on them, a silence which neither wants to break. This moment of communion becomes a moment of unity where two people are one in humility, in the gift of self to the other. It is a moment of eternity in a world where people are usually caught up in action, noise, aggression, a quest for efficiency, and the need to prove themselves. Two hearts beat together, each giving the other freedom. Each person is fully present to the other. It is as if time stands still. And yet nobody can find everything they need in one other person. The child grows and discovers new people and the world; the mother needs her husband, her own work, as well as her baby. The other person is not God; he or she cannot completely satisfy the human heart. He or she is perhaps an instrument of God, revealing God's presence. Moments of peace, contemplation and communion deepen and widen the human heart; they show that it is possible to be more, to live more, to search more, to love more and to give of oneself more. They are moments of fulfilment, but also new beginnings.

Communion is not only a moment of sacred silence between two people; it can also be present in an atmosphere, an attitude and a way of living and being among others. It exists, for example, in groups of people who come together to sing, play, celebrate and pray; or among people living far away from one another who know that they are united by bonds of love. Of course, these bonds need to be renewed and nourished from time to time, but they endure despite time and distance.

Communion and weakness

Communion seems linked to weakness and to vulnerability. When people are enjoying success they look above all for admiration, but when they feel weak they seek communion. This weakness can be that of small children or elderly people, those who are sick or who have been injured, people who have suffered a professional set-back or have a handicap, people suffering from depression. When they find themselves in a weak state, they do not want elaborate discussions or actions. They want to be with someone who is close to them, who takes their hand and says, 'I am happy to be with you.' Then they know that they are loved not for what they are capable of doing, but for who they are. It is then that they begin to regain confidence in themselves. And the heart of a capable, strong person is opened up and touched by the call of love from the weaker person.

When I see a beggar in the street or in the Metro, I tend to put my hand into my pocket and give him the first coin that I find there. It might be a franc, or two francs, fifty centimes or ten francs. As I give it to him, I look into his eyes and say a few words to him. As our eyes meet, there seems to be a moment of communion and of mutual understanding between us which brings me peace. Other people in the Metro avoid looking at me, they even seem frightened if I look at them. If I try to meet their eyes, they become suspicious that I am trying to make a pass at them, or that I want to steal something from them. Everyone seems scared of others, but the beggar is not – maybe because he has nothing to lose. I can look at him. He is not afraid of me, and I am not afraid of him. And this simple look can give him back a little confidence in himself. Maybe it can give me confidence in myself too. Every man who loses confidence in himself, who has fallen into the world of alcohol or drugs, or who has failed in family life or relationships or work needs someone who looks at him as a human being, with tenderness and trust. And it is this moment of communion which enables him, little by little, to rebuild his confidence. When someone tells you about his success and prowess, you admire him. But when he shares with you his weakness, his faults and his difficulties, he elicits your compassion. Humility leads to and creates communion.

The fruits of communion

A baby girl lying in the arms of her mother or father, playing with them, smiling and laughing, is an icon of happiness. Her body relaxes, her face shines, her eyes twinkle, her hands wave in love. She senses that she is loved, and so she knows that she is someone; she is alive. She is not alone. Despite her weakness and littleness, she has no need to defend herself. Because she is loved, she is safe. She is secure, peaceful. She can live and love. All her being is united in and through this communion. She becomes whole.

This is the fruit of communion. This communion which brings a moment of happiness, shapes the depths of the child's psychology. It allows her to move through life with confidence in herself, in others and in the world. When I visit hospitals, I love to take children who have severe handicaps into my arms. Abandoned to their solitude behind the bars of their little cots, they sit there with vacant eyes and sad expressions. I open my coat and take the little baby girl in my arms and hug her body against mine so that she can feel the warmth of my body and my heartbeat. Immediately, her body begins to respond, her arms reach out with joy, she starts to laugh. It reminds me of a thirsty man in a desert who comes upon an oasis and starts to drink madly, splashing water on his face, laughing with joy. The child thirsts for communion, without it she dies. The thirst for communion is at the heart of our existence.

I have already spoken of the man whom I met shouting in the Metro in Paris. I was sitting down and I waited for him to approach. Suddenly, I saw a begging hand held out in front of me. I took it, and squeezed it. I looked at this young man's face. He was barely twenty-five years old, dirty, unshaven. His clothes stank. I asked him his name and where he was from, smiled at him and slipped a one-franc piece into his hand. He looked at me with tenderness, his eyes filled with real gentleness. He saw that I was not feeling too good myself, because I was tired. He said: 'We are both in the same boat, you and I!' Then he left, shouting angrily at everyone. It seemed to me that the way he looked at me came from the very deepest part of his being. He longed for a name, and to be seen as a human being.

Obviously, this was just a fleeting moment of communion, but it was a moment which revealed the thirst that every human being has for communion. I do not think I would be able to live day after day with that man. His thirst could never be quenched; he was filled with anguish which he expressed through anger. I suspect that as a tiny child he never knew the loving presence of a mother and father. He was searching constantly for a tenderness which he had never known, and which he will probably never be able to find. Today, his longing for communion is conveyed through his angry shouting. But that moment of communion awoke also what was deepest in me.

The desire in the heart of every human being is to find communion and tenderness, a feeling of loving and being loved through a physical presence. This thirst for communion seems to be one of the most important ingredients in sexual desire. But the fear of commitment and of true love can be so strong that this thirst can bring people to sexual acts which are cut off from true love and commitment, and are no longer an expression of them. The desire for communion then remains unfulfilled. These sexual acts can quickly become a game, a need to possess, seduce or conquer someone, or to seek our own pleasure. They can also become sadistic, driven by the need to hurt someone. Experiences which are potentially the most beautiful can become the saddest and most wounding. Love and hate seem so close.

Real communion is difficult. It implies a choice, commitment, gentleness, trust and a respect for the other and for his or her freedom. Communion is the gift of self, and through this gift comes immense joy and even a form of ecstasy.

Little by little, we human beings discover our inability to fulfil our deep thirst for communion. This inability springs from our fear of love, which finds its source in our own wounded and broken hearts and in the wounded and broken hearts of others. But how has the heart in each of us become wounded and broken?

2 Origin of the wound

My friends Robert and Susan were expecting their first child. From the sixth month of the pregnancy, knowing that the baby would now be starting to hear, Robert began to sing a song to the little one every evening. He was present at the birth of Diane who, like all newborn babies, howled in distress. He began to sing the song he had sung to her every evening. Diane immediately stopped crying and turned her head towards her father. She recognised his voice. The child begins her life in her mother's womb. This is a peaceful, safe place in which there is also some communication. The child in the womb can feel whether her mother is tense or relaxed. At a certain stage in her development, she can hear the music of her mother's voice. But one day, the womb becomes too small; the child then lives the trauma and anguish of birth. From this safe, secure, warm haven, she is plunged into a world of infinite horizons. She is no longer enveloped, directly nourished from her mother's blood. She is in contact with light and air. She lives the anguish of isolation and of the unknown, but happily all this ends in the arms of her mother. She discovers her mother's tenderness and the softness of her body, she rests on her breast, she discovers her delicate and loving touch. This tiny, newborn baby is very fragile, very small; she can do nothing by herself. All alone, she is in danger of dying. She cannot feed, wash or dress herself. If she feels cold, she cannot pull blankets over herself. The baby is totally helpless. All she can do is cry for help and show her joy.

After the trauma of birth, the tiny child will begin to feel discomfort. She will feel hungry and will cry. And her mother will respond by offering her her breast; she will feed her. Discomfort is then transformed into peace and a feeling of fullness and contentment. The child discovers that there is someone who responds to her cry. She is protected and loved; she discovers communion and trust in another. And each time she cries, her mother is there. Through an extraordinary maternal instinct, the mother understands her child's cry; she knows whether she is hungry, tired, ill, lonely ... The child senses that her desires and difficulties are understood. Despite – or perhaps because of – her weakness, she is at peace, she is not afraid because she is loved. She discovers that her mother pays special attention to her and she gradually comes to realise that she is absolutely unique. She is the most beautiful child in the world! She is at the centre of the family, giving immense joy to her mother, father, uncles, aunts, grandparents. Obviously, the child's consciousness of this communion is not on a rational level, as she can neither conceptualise nor verbalise it. But she feels the special attention, enveloped in tenderness and kindness, that is given her. It is this love that forms the base of her being. This love is like a message, revealing to the tiny child her value and importance. Her heart and her body open up to it. She is living in a communion of trust with her mother, which enables her to build communion with her father, brothers and sisters and other members of the family. These will lead her on into communion with air, light, earth and water. The world is not a hostile but a friendly place.

But in some circumstances, the child becomes aware that

the mother does not want her. She cannot respond to her cry. She gets cross and she talks in an irritated tone. Her body is tense and her voice is no longer gentle and melodious but aggressive. All parents have their weaknesses and emotional wounds. There are times when they feel tired and depressed, overcome by work or by anxieties. No human being can remain constantly in a state of welcome and communion. The mother is taken up with other things – maybe she has work to do, or she has other children to care for, or she has had an argument with her husband, and so she does not manage to enfold her child in love as she would wish to. The child finds that Mummy no longer seems to want her as she did before.

I have often been struck at l'Arche, when a little boy has started to run about during a community event, by how his mother then becomes anxious, runs towards her son and falls on him like a vulture on its prey. She seizes him and carries him away upset and confused. Perhaps this happens partly because of the mother's own wounds. Perhaps she is afraid of being seen as a weak mother who is bringing up her child badly. But the child cannot understand the aggressive attitude of his mother. He wandered off by himself in a spirit of curiosity, wanting to find things out. He was enjoying moving and walking and running by himself, but suddenly she rushed at him, whisking him away.

A child's cry of anguish frequently provokes anguish in the parents. They discover that they are often helpless before him. The child then does more than disturb, he brings forth anguish and violence; above all at night when he keeps them awake for long hours with his crying. The child in turn experiences terror and panic, feeling his parents' aggression turned towards him. In order to survive, he develops a kind of anger which enables him to overcome this fear and guilt; or else he may turn this against himself by falling into depression.

The different sources of wounds of the heart

In our community in the Philippines, we welcomed Helen, a young, very small, fifteen-year-old girl. She was blind and her body was all twisted, she could not move her arms and legs. She had been put in a hospital when she was a small child. Keiko, a Japanese assistant, looked after her with great love and care, but she admitted to me that it was difficult. Helen was totally closed in on herself and gave no sign of either joy or anger. She was completely apathetic. Keiko and I chatted about depression in children, and I encouraged her to carry on loving Helen, talking to her gently, singing to her and touching her tenderly. 'Hopefully one day she will smile at you,' I said, and I made her promise to send me a postcard when this happened. Some months later, a postcard arrived: 'Helen smiled at me today, Love, Keiko.'

When a child like Helen no longer lives in communion with her mother and father, when she finds herself alone, she is plunged into loneliness and anguish. Anguish is something very difficult for a child to deal with. It is a chaotic energy, with no particular focus, that surges up within the body; it is agitation and malaise. It can take away the appetite and disturb sleep patterns; it plunges the child into confusion and destroys inner peace and unity. If the child feels neither loved nor wanted, this anguish and loneliness quickly turns into guilt or shame: if she is not loved, then she is not lovable; she is bad. She feels that she is the object of anger, she becomes convinced that there is something wrong with her, and she begins to want to hurt others. It is too much for her.

She cannot cope with the inner pain, anguish and feelings of guilt.

The child experiences the same kind of anguish when her mother is too possessive, when the mother or father tries to suppress her desires and freedom, when they wish to control her and use her to fill a void in themselves. The child then feels suffocated, crushed. Her mother's touch becomes ambiguous; it is the touch of possession, and not a touch which brings security and life. This kind of false communion is sometimes even more dangerous than rejection, and gives rise to serious tensions in the child.

When we, as adults, feel this anguish rising up inside us, we have lots of ways of distracting ourselves: we can throw ourselves into work, watch television, ring up a friend, pick up a book, go jogging or for a walk, go out to the pub for a drink . . . We have a multitude of things which enable us to put aside and forget our feelings of anguish. But what can a child do? Nothing. His body becomes filled with anguish. He cries. His cries may perhaps cause his parents to react with even greater anger, and then there is a vicious circle in which the child's anguish provokes anguish in the parents, and the parents' anguish increases that in the child.

When I say that the child does not know how to defend herself, it is true; but it is not the whole truth. She cannot throw herself into work, nor phone a friend for a chat, but she finds other ways to protect herself, and in doing so runs the risk of damaging herself psychologically. She can withdraw into herself, like little Helen; refusing to communicate and cutting herself off emotionally. She can sulk. In one way or another, we have all had experiences like this, where we have been pushed down by somebody, and either we have withdrawn into ourselves, or alternatively we have become angry. The only thing that could help Helen emerge from her inner prison was the unconditional love of Keiko, who said to her: 'I love you just as you are. I do not judge you, I am not angry with you, I love you.' Little by little, Helen dared to trust her.

A child can also protect herself by escaping into dreams. She then enters into a completely imaginary world so as to avoid the pain of reality: the reality of her own body and anguish, the reality of broken communion, the reality of a sick and depressed mother or an angry father. All this pain and fear are too much for her. Dreams are an extraordinary protection against suffering and reality. So the child creates her own world sheltered from pain, sheltered particularly from inner pain. The child can also hide behind competitive games, where she can prove herself, instead of games of communion. Little by little she freezes her emotions – blocking off the inner pain of loneliness and broken communion.

When the child discovers that communion is difficult and a source of suffering, or that it does not exist, she lives a kind of inner death. She feels worthless and useless. It is then that guilt is born. This is the most painful thing a child can experience, and it is without doubt a feeling deeply rooted in each of us, because we have all lived this moment of broken communion which gives rise to anguish and guilt. Psychologists call it 'shame', but I prefer to keep the word 'guilt': if we feel we are not loved, it seems that it must be because we are bad, guilty of something. Obviously, it is a psychological rather than a moral guilt. This is how self-confidence is broken in the child. This feeling of guilt will reassert itself throughout her life, creating in her a broken self-image.

This guilt can become even greater when a child develops anger and a desire for vengeance against her parents. Her rage is a sign of life, but it also makes her afraid. She discovers a wolf inside herself, capable of killing and doing harm. This feeling reinforces her guilt. She screams out: 'I do not want love! I hate love! I hate Mummy! I hate Daddy! I hate my little brother! I am going to smash up his toys!' The world is no longer a place of communion; it is a hostile place. The child has to defend herself against the forces attacking her, so she becomes aggressive, she counter-attacks. As some psychologists have shown, fairy tales are necessary to help a child to exorcise the wolf hidden in her.

Even more serious than anger and aggression in a child who is defending herself is sheer guilt. The child then seeks to damage and hurt herself; she is the person at fault, she is thoroughly bad. She turns her anger against herself in self-destructive acts.

Possessive love

At l'Arche, we have welcomed certain men and women with handicaps who were victims of their anguished mothers. Often, their fathers were absent; the mother was strong and dominant. She filled up her inner emptiness and feeling of loneliness and uselessness by doing everything for her child. She thought of herself as loving, because her life was completely devoted to her child, but in fact she was stifling him. She was unable to listen to his wishes, to help him to develop and grow to greater independence. Was there perhaps some unconscious desire that the child should remain dependent so that through him she could feel she was a good mother and no longer be lonely? Curbing a child's freedom through excessive affection is sometimes even worse than abandoning him. A mother who behaves like this knows how to manipulate her child by playing on his feelings of guilt or his desire for immediate rewards. Symbiotic and suffocating communion then develops. But this is not true communion.

I remember a young girl called Alix who was an assistant at l'Arche. I asked her what her childhood was like. She told me she was from a loving family, and that she and her parents got on very well together. Her family was religious, very well thought of by the church authorities. Then I asked her what subjects she had studied. She told me. I asked her why she had chosen those particular ones. She replied, 'It was my Mum who wanted me to do those subjects.' The longer the conversation went on, the more I realised that she had done everything that her mother wanted. She had absolutely no idea who she was or what she wanted. I am afraid that she will probably have great difficulty in entering into any real relationship and communion during her life because of the manipulative ways of her mother. It was clear that her mother wanted to control her completely and through her to achieve all those things that she had not been able to achieve herself. This young girl was in fact deeply wounded, and with one of the most serious – and sadly most common – wounds, that of false communion. This prevents someone like Alix from existing and being able to take her life into her own hands, to become what she is really called to be, a free woman. The whole idea of love can become dangerous for Alix because it seems to prevent her existing.

One young woman assistant at l'Arche became particularly attached to Marie-Pierre, a woman with a severe handicap. She wanted to take her on holiday, and to sleep in the same room as her. Then we began to be aware that she was jealous if others gave Marie-Pierre her bath. At first, Marie-Pierre was delighted with all this attention. But then, little by little, she seemed to lose a certain joy and spontaneity. Relationships like this become unhealthy, for they are closed and lack freedom and joy. Some false communions inspired by insecurity and fear can fill an inner void and calm anguish; and in this way can become addictive. This is no longer communion built on trust and giving freedom.

Deceitful love

Not long ago, I was talking with a psychologist in charge of a ward for so-called 'chronic schizophrenics' (this is not a term I like) in a psychiatric hospital. The psychologist said to me, 'It's astonishing. I have discovered that all the schizophrenics in my charge were sexually abused as children.' What is sexual abuse? Dad is often angry, he is difficult, he does not listen to his children. And then there is that uncle who is gentle, who awakens the heart, who touches affectionately and who gives presents. But one day, his touch becomes a sexual touch. He finds sexual pleasure in his nephew or niece's body, and tries to arouse sexual pleasure in them. Then he says to them: 'If you say anything about this to your mother or father, I will kill you.' And so the child discovers a perverse new form of 'communion'; the child who was happy when the 'kind' uncle was present suddenly realises that communion is dangerous, that love is false. A breakage takes place in the child's heart. His greatest desire – communion – becomes the most dangerous, for it could lead to death.

These same fears take hold of a child when he is surrounded by conflict, when his mother and father separate and each tries to get him on his or her side and to win him over with presents. The child's heart is wounded, divided. He is confused. But he can also profit from this situation by obtaining more possessions.

Division wounds him but it can also serve him, or rather his egotistical needs.

The fear of loving

When wounds, anguish and guilt erupt in the heart of a little boy, he will try to escape into another inner world, trying to avoid or forget all the inner pain. He hides it all away in secret parts of his being as if it had never existed. But the world of suffering stays hidden within him, like a malignant cancer. And so a wall grows up between his conscious world and the place where he has stuffed away all he wants to forget – which becomes the unconscious world. Sometimes this wall is thick; it takes the form of a pyschosis which seems to have its origins not only in a psychological disorder but also in the biological make-up of the person. This wall is not only a sickness, it is also a protection; without it the child would probably have died of anguish and fear.

How strong and beautiful life is! No matter how much we suffer, and despite our inner walls, this vital energy continues to circulate. The child grows, he develops; he has to live and to survive. He needs to overcome these feelings of inner death. His energies are no longer directed towards relationships and communion; these have become too dangerous for him and cause too much pain. They are diverted instead towards acquisitions and activities through which he can find pleasure and prove his worth to himself, his parents and his friends and so be admired by them.

And this pain appears in the heart of every human being as an ambivalence towards love. We yearn for communion, to be very close to another human being in a permanent way, but at the same time we are frightened. Because the child has experienced happiness through communion, at least for a moment, communion seems to be the place of human fulfilment and happiness. But it seems also to be a place of death, fear and guilt, because the child has known broken communion and false communion – emotional manipulation and possession which stifled his being and his freedom. Other people then appear to be dangerous.

And so the human being is pretty well forced to turn away from communion and to direct his energies elsewhere. He denies communion; it is not possible. It becomes a game where we manipulate others for our own well-being. Sartre, in *Being and Nothingness*, asserts that love is a mirage, created by an evil spirit. It looks like happiness, but in fact to love is to devour someone; it is conquest, one person's freedom feeding off another's.

So is communion possible? Is it a mirage created by an evil spirit, or is it the dwelling place of God? This is the question that faces the human being who searches for unity, peace, freedom, light and love, but who loses heart because of all the opposing forces within and around him.

The need to be the best

Every human being – and I mean every single one – has experienced this broken, false or impossible communion. Inside each one of us is a hidden world of suffering, death and guilt. Some people are much more wounded than others. But there is a connection between those who live with failure – the down-and-out, the alcoholic, the destitute, the depressive – and those who work unstintingly for personal success, or even for great causes: company directors, politicians, film-stars, dissidents, heroes of all sorts. Despite appearances, and despite all kinds of variations, their psychological make-up is similar. In one lot of people, the inner wounds or brokenness have led to drink, degeneration and depression, in the sense that they are victims; in the others the same inner wounds or brokenness have bred a kind of urgent need to be successful, to dominate, to be well known, even to save others – they need to establish an identity through being admired and powerful. Some are addicted to drink, others to work.

This inner dis-ease, this guilt and feeling of worthlessness, is like a motor which propels a human being into frenetic activity in an effort to make up for this feeling of guilt and to prove to himself that he is part of an élite, that he is one of the best. This need to win, to climb the ladder of human promotion can begin in childhood and continue for the whole of somebody's life. If a child comes first in class or does well in sport, he knows that his parents will be pleased. His position will then be secure. The constant striving for success and this need to win, to prove oneself, render communion and true relationships difficult, if not impossible.

A broken self-image is a personal reality caused by sufferings in the relationship between a child and his parents. It is also a cultural and sociological reality, partly transmitted through the parents' suffering and through culture. There are groups of oppressed people who have always been looked down upon on account of their nationality, race, religion, or class. This contempt affects the image they have of themselves; they feel ashamed of being who they are, ashamed of their race or of their class.

The inner wall

Thanks to the psychological wall around our hearts, we can hide and forget the reality of our wounds and our fundamental poverty. We can live and survive and avoid being plunged into a world of depression or rebellion. Thus we advance along the road of life gathering possessions and seeking recognition . . . unless the walls are not strong enough, and then we languish in depression and cynicism.

Behind the wall, buried in the subconscious, there are not only negative things produced by broken communion, but also the fundamental quest for true communion, and latent energies made for love. Behind the wall lies not only what is most wounded and dark in human beings, but also what is most beautiful. There is the potential for joy and love, but also a terrible fear of love and of the suffering associated with love. The point of departure from which we act is often this wall and not the source of our being. The wall becomes that aggressive ego seeking recognition, which controls our acts and subtly avoids everything that threatens to make us fail or to belittle us. This is how our actions become imprinted with a kind of fierce egoism of which we cannot rid ourselves. We do everything to prove ourselves, to boost our image, to gain glory. The greatest fear in human beings is of not existing, or of being brought down, judged, condemned, rejected as someone bad. In some ways, philosophers who take a pessimistic view of human nature have a point: human beings are constantly fighting to achieve success and admiration at any price – even when that involves trampling on others on the way.

This wall cuts human beings off from their true source. They are no longer like animals, birds, fish and plants that grow and give life moving from their own centre of life. Animals do not wear masks; they are not conditioned by a need to succeed, to be congratulated and admired, or by a fear of rejection. Each of them lives in a simple, uncomplicated way. Obviously, they are afraid of danger, but they seem to be able to live confidently that which they are. It seems that a wounded heart stops a person from being able to live simply as him- or herself. The human being then becomes a competitive creature, who seeks to prove that he is part of an élite and who hides his limitations, or else he victimises himself, accusing others if they do not fulfil his needs. Cut off from his true source, he is cut off from the source of the universe. He no longer acts out of love for the world, but out of a need to protect and prove himself.

This wall is the starting point for all the activities of strength and power and knowledge which enable the human being to be satisfied with himself. He is strengthened with the defence mechanisms which surround his vulnerability. There are businessmen so caught up in their deals that they are unable to listen to their wives and children. They are unable even to understand the sufferings and needs of others. They are closed behind their projects, the only things that make them feel alive. If this wall cuts us all from our own true source, it also prevents us from perceiving reality as it is. We tend to perceive it as we would like it to be. This renders us all partially blind, highly selective, and incapable of seeing and accepting ourselves and others as they are; it is the source of all our prejudices.

Walls, morals, choices

Each individual's experiences of life determine how closed and solid this wall will be. It is not a wall made of bricks. It is a psychological wall behind which is hidden everything that the child has not been able to cope with. It is rather like a dirty window which just about lets light shine through it. Children and adolescents, using their intelligence and supported by a good upbringing, know that there are things that are good to do – helping up an old woman who has fallen on the ground, for example – and things that should not be done, like taking things that belong to someone else.

They have learned from their first relationship with their mother, from this first communion, that their mother is a person who feels joy and pain and has needs, who has a heart that can be wounded. And so they come to know that each human being is precious, and that it is important to respect everyone. This inspires them to kindness and generosity, especially if they have been brought up surrounded by goodness. They can then choose to work for goodness, justice, truth and light. But they can equally choose to take a different route, to be attracted by other things. But even if they direct themselves towards good works, they risk being driven by the need to be admired and affirmed by others. There is always this instrinsic egoism, this need to be known and thought well of.

Some children have simply suffered too much. The barriers around their hearts are too solid; their need for attention, for the loving parents they have never had is too strong. Their fears and angers are too immense. They have been made to protect themselves too much. Perhaps one day they may have an experience – a sudden intuition or an experience of God – which will help them to discover that communion and love do exist. Then they will know they are loved just as they are. Perhaps this will be through a chance meeting with a social worker, a prison visitor, a fellow prisoner, a chaplain – someone who sees the good in them. This will be a revelation. The psychological wall is not immovable; it can evolve and change. It can gradually be weakened so that the person becomes in touch with the source of his or her being.

Behind the wall: the hidden world of the subconscious

This repressed world which is made up of all that the child was not able to cope with remains hidden in the depths of the human being. Consciousness and memory have no access to it. It all seems to have been forgotten. Yet it continues to control behaviour in several ways. It is revealed in difficulties in relationships, and in a fear of being abandoned, crushed or suffocated by authority. It may be revealed also in an inability to find the right distance in relationships; perhaps we get too close to people, or we keep too distant from them. It is also manifested in an inability to see and understand the needs of others, in moments of madness or depression, or in bursts of irrational anger against certain people.

Behind the wall, there is a world of anguish which we are afraid of, and which we therefore refuse to look at. We cannot accept the pain, weaknesses, fears and guilt that are hidden there. We deny the existence of a certain part of ourselves, the part where we have been wounded and where we remain fragile and weak. The same impulse that makes us ignore the existence of poor people and people in distress makes us disown the poor and distressed person within ourselves. The great walls that surround us on the outside have their origin in this inner separation. The filth of shanty towns and prisons is a reflection of the filth inside ourselves. So how can we learn to embrace not only the poverty around us but also within us?

3 Difficulties in relationships

The deep wound or brokenness in the hearts of human beings, and the psychological walls built around them as protection, are painfully obvious in our relationships with others. We like to surround ourselves with people who flatter us, think well of us, need us and admire our gifts. But we tend to avoid those who do not recognise our value, do not admire us nor trust us, are afraid of us, judge us or even push us down. They perceive our weaknesses, even though we have carefully constructed masks and images to hide them.

Looking back, I can see that when I was in the navy I was preoccupied with success and with trying to win the admiration of my superiors. I loved the spirit and power that came with naval life. Efficiency, not people, was my first concern. Similarly, when I left the navy, it was not primarily *people* who interested me. I wanted to devote myself to an *ideal* of peace and Christian life, and to the study of philosophy and theology. Certainly, I wanted to follow Jesus, to know him and love him, but more out of idealism than because I wanted to live communion. It took me some time to discover all my inner brokenness which provoked difficulties in relationships, and a fear of others. I was happy to command, teach, obey and learn; but entering into communion with others, making myself vulnerable by forming relationships with them, was far more difficult. I avoided people by throwing my energy into doing good things, praying and studying. But maybe that was a necessary time of growth for me. I needed the spiritual and intellectual formation which would gradually give me the inner strength to be able to enter into real relationships, to learn to listen to people and love them, and to become really myself. Even today, I have difficulties in communicating with people, in not hiding myself behind an ideal. I can easily retreat into myself; the walls inside me are still solid, even though slowly they are becoming a little less solid – it is a lifetime's work! There are undoubtedly great vulnerabilities and fears hidden behind these walls. I often notice anger and a certain defensiveness welling up in me when I am in discussion with someone who holds intellectual, political, social, philosophical or religious views that are different from mine, especially if there is no communion or friendship that binds us together. I can even feel the tone of my voice changing. It is no longer a tone of welcome, openness, listening and tenderness, but a lower, more aggressive tone. Where do these defence mechanisms come from? Do they spring from a fear of being shown to be wrong, of being at fault, of being criticised? Fear that the other person is touching irrational prejudices within me? Fear that they might think that I am closed in an ideology which serves my purposes?

I sometimes experience within me a tremendous energy which is more like anguish or agitation and which incites me to do things, to organise projects, to control people. My inner motor seems to be in overdrive. It is then quite difficult for me to slow down, to be still, to be open and welcoming toward others, to make myself vulnerable to them, to be peaceful and silent. I do not always know the causes of this anguish; they may be physical, psychological, or spiritual. But that chaotic energy is there, urging me to do things without knowing why. Action seems to calm the inner pain. Yet communion at these times is rendered almost impossible. When I am in this state, I understand people who suffer from psychosis. When we are suffering too much inner anguish and confusion, we are forced to cut ourselves off from other people, push them away and hide behind barriers. Yet this seems to increase the anguish, and it reveals our total inability to relate. At other moments, my head is buzzing with so many ideas and plans, that I am unable to really see others and their needs.

Judgment which causes separation

I was once present at a meeting when someone described the difficulties he had in forming relationships. 'When I see the other people's failings,' he said, 'I judge and criticise and belittle them. I feel superior. But when I meet someone who makes me feel inferior, I see all the gifts and talents that they have and I don't, and I become jealous. Then I want to get close to them, to take their gifts and use them for my own benefit. I have real difficulty in entering into equal relationships where I can give and receive.'

We are so quick to judge others! We have such an astonishing capacity to see their failings, and such difficulty in recognising and accepting our own. By being judgmental, we separate ourselves from others; we build walls between ourselves and them. We think we are better, superior to them. All of us are without doubt frightened of those who, through their presence, qualities, attitudes and words, reveal our limits and our faults to us and lower our self-esteem. These people touch our inner wounds, awakening our guilt. We have to pre-empt the judgment of such people by criticising them and keeping well away from them.

I always marvel at those penetrating words of Jesus: 'Do not try to take the splinter from someone else's eye when you have a plank in your own. Fool! Take the plank from your own eye, and then you will be able to see clearly to take the splinter from the other person's' (Matt. 7:3–5). We are all the same. It is easy to see another's weaknesses and faults, but a psychological wall prevents us from seeing our own. Each of us has a plank in our own eye, which blinds us to our faults. Or if we do perceive them, we fall into depression! The walls we create to protect our vulnerability prevent us seeing and accepting reality as it is – it is too painful. It is much easier to live in illusions, dreams and ideologies, seeing the world and people as we want them to be, rather than as they are.

The fear of opening our hearts to others

Superficial relationships are easy. We discuss politics, cooking, sport. It is a way of passing the time, of filling the void. We do things together: play sport, go for a walk, go to the cinema. We work together or collaborate in religious, political or social projects. But the doors of our hearts can remain firmly closed. We do not really allow others to get close to us. We do not open ourselves to them. We do not become vulnerable to them. We do not show them who we really are. Above all, we keep our vulnerability and fragility hidden.

This can also be true in professional activities and in charitable work. We do things for others, often good things. We teach them, care for them, give them money. But our hearts remain closed. We remain in a position of control and superiority. Sometimes, certainly, it is necessary to behave like this. A doctor, for example, cannot burden all her patients with her problems; she has a job to do. But on the other hand, the doctor who cannot really listen, who fails to perceive the anguish and deep suffering of her patients, who has no time to welcome them as they are and to understand them, cannot be a good doctor. Someone who remains on a professional pedestal, welcoming others only in her head, refusing to welcome them in her heart and with compassion, cannot really care for them properly. If we are to be truly compassionate, we must allow ourselves to be touched by others, by their suffering, by the cry of their being. Patients then perceive that they are understood and loved as they are, they begin to open their hearts and to trust. It is probable then that healing will come more quickly. But true compassion demands time, patience, listening; it demands the capacity to accept each person just as they are, whether they are poor or rich, grateful or ungrateful, friend or stranger; whether or not they feel like kindred spirits. Then the whole person is being treated, and not just an illness or a part of their body.

We have all met men and women who are completely consumed by their work. They appear hard, but in fact are brittle and hide behind their capability, ideas and books. They are unable to listen to others and above all unable to enter into communion with them. What are they afraid of? Why do they keep their distance from people? Why does relationship disturb them? Why do they have this fear that if they enter into relationship they will be manipulated, crushed, suffocated, or lose their power to control what is happening? They have been forced to defend themselves by using walls to create a fortress against relationships which to them seem like invasions.

Communion is dangerous for people who feel themselves to be weak, fragile and insecure. They are afraid that if a person approaches them with kindness, he or she will soon touch what is broken in them and will then reject them. They cannot bear the idea of living through another experience of abandonment and rejection, and so it seems better to put up fortress-like walls and avoid relationships than to risk suffering another abandonment. Others are afraid of entering into relationships because they are afraid of losing control of a situation, afraid of inspiring in others a desire to get close to them, which would stifle their freedom and independence. They are afraid of losing power and of being swallowed up by the vacuum in another, by their insatiable need to be loved.

Equally, relationships can seem dangerous because of the links between communion and sexuality. Some men avoid women because they have not really integrated their own sexuality. Women seem to awaken in them their immense, seemingly uncontrollable need for communion and tenderness. They feel forced to hide behind walls of knowledge and power. They tend either to denigrate women, or to put them on pedestals, rendering them untouchable. The same thing happens with women who are, consciously or unconsciously, looking for love and tenderness. They keep away from men because they lack a certain inner strength which would enable them to keep the right distance in relationships. They keep away from them too perhaps because they have had negative experiences with men who were looking for a sexual relationship, or a kind of communion-possession, more than true relationship.

Other people throw themselves into relationships, but only superficial ones. There will be sharing and floods of words, even intimate physical relations, but they cannot really engage in relationship because they are too conscious of their own wounds and of being unlovable. Are they afraid of the suffering that might ensue if they were truly committed to another? Are they afraid of opening themselves to another and so losing a certain freedom and independence? Somebody told me recently about a woman, very successful professionally, who had decided never to enter into a relationship with a man, not to waste her time with matters of the heart. Was she afraid of becoming vulnerable to another, and opening her heart to him and then losing her professional identity? Had she lived bad experiences of manipulative, possessive or stifling love during childhood? Entering into the to-and-fro of communion is dangerous. To open our heart and then be rejected or possessed is terribly painful. But perhaps this woman was afraid that she was unable to love? Did she lack confidence in herself? Was she afraid of abandoning herself to love and of being forced to take a path she did not necessarily want, and where she would lose control? Is it not better then to block ourselves off from this emotional world which we cannot always control? In the world of relationships, there is never complete security. And whatever happens, all relationships end, at least physically, at death. Death is that horrible and absolute separation. That woman's decision is understandable. But at the same time, by closing in on herself and her work, she was cutting herself off from the most beautiful thing in human life: the communion of hearts. What if one day she loses her job, or finds herself unable to work because of age or illness, then what will be left for her? Friendship is risky, but is life not risky too? Is friendship not a gift that is given to us when we are in good health, but which is above all for when we become weaker and in need?

There are also people who are constantly seeking tenderness. If they are not the objects of loving attention, they are overcome by anguish, they no longer feel alive. It is difficult to live real communion with them because they tend to manipulate others, or even to develop psychosomatic illnessess to attract attention to themselves.

The fear of the cry of the poor

One day in Paris, I was accosted by a woman. 'Give me ten francs,' she said. I stopped and asked, 'Why do you need ten francs?' To which she replied, 'I haven't eaten anything all day.' When I asked why not, she began to talk to me. She had recently been released from a psychiatric hospital. She told me a little about her life and her family. Suddenly I realised that the conversation was becoming quite serious, and that if I continued talking to this woman I might pass the point of no return; I would become obliged to spend time with her, probably a lot of time. I became frightened. I gave her ten francs and left.

What lay behind my fear? This was a woman with immense needs, in grave personal difficulty and anguish, a single woman who had probably often been abandoned. She needed a lot of my time and I had a meeting to get to. So often we use our plans and projects as an excuse for not helping a person in dire need. This is what the priest and the Levite did in the parable of the Good Samaritan (Luke 10:30–5); and it is what I did too. But perhaps my apprehension sprung also from a fear that I would never be able to fulfil all her needs. Perhaps what this woman needed was a man who would be father, mother, social worker, friend, brother and husband all at once. Her cry for love was like a bottomless chasm, the cry of the small child within her howling for her father and mother who probably had abandoned or mistreated her. I was possibly afraid that my life would be swallowed up in the immense chasm of her needs, afraid that I would lose my freedom, identity and being. Perhaps also I simply did not want to be bothered;

I had my own problems and difficulties. I did not want to open myself to the sufferings of another. Perhaps she was afraid too. Perhaps she was asking herself who was this man who was gradually entering into a relationship with her and taking her seriously. Perhaps she had already been deceived thousands of times by men. Perhaps she panicked at the prospect of a relationship, fearing that the other person would discover what an awful person she was and would then abandon her, yet again. Perhaps we were both subject to the two deepest kinds of fear in the human psyche: on her part, the fear of being abandoned; on mine, the fear of being swallowed up by a relationship, and of losing my freedom and creativity.

Relationships which provoke anguish

One sad experience at l'Arche revealed very powerfully to me the world of shadows inside myself. It concerned Lucien, a man with a serious handicap. He is paralysed, he cannot speak, walk or look after himself and he is incontinent. For thirty years he lived with his mother who looked after him with great patience and tenderness. She understood him. She knew how to interpret his smallest gesture or cry; and she responded with wisdom and love. As his father had died when he was young, she was the only person who had touched him for thirty years. One day, the mother was sent to hospital. Lucien had to be hospitalised too because there was no one to look after him. He had no idea what was going on. He was suddenly separated from the one he loved; plunged into a world of appalling distress. Sensing that he had been abandoned, he howled in anguish. This is how he came to be at l'Arche. I met him when I lived in the house called 'La Forestière' which had welcomed Eric and Lucien and eight other people with severe handicaps.

Sometimes, Lucien would enter into this world of anguish. Nobody knew exactly what brought on these terrible moods, but he used to howl as if he would never stop. His cries of anguish were very high-pitched; they pierced me like a sword. I could not bear them. Perhaps they reawoke all the pain and anguish of my own childhood, hidden away behind all the barriers in me. And this anguish in me became anger and violence and hate. I would have liked to have killed Lucien, to have hurled him out of the window. I would have liked to have run away, but I could not because I had responsibilities in the house. I was filled with shame and guilt and confusion.

Obviously, because I was surrounded by other assistants, I did not harm Lucien or hit him. But I began to understand how it is that many children are admitted to hospital in a serious state, having been battered by their mothers or fathers. A mother on her own, with two or three children, abandoned by her husband, depressive, beset with difficulties in her life and work, is terribly insecure and fragile. She cannot respond to her children and give them the tenderness they need because her emotional resources have been exhausted. She is empty. She becomes exasperated by the children crying out for love. She cannot stand it anymore; her anguish becomes violence, and she hits a child. And then she bursts into tears realising what a horrible thing she has done.

There are also people who provoke anguish in another simply through their presence and without meaning to at all. They call forth a world of darkness from within the other. A woman who is frustrated because she has never been loved as a woman, who has had to put all her energies into a career, may find it difficult to put up with a pretty young girl surrounded by admirers. All the career woman's shortcomings and deepest needs which she has been obliged to suppress are suddenly exposed. Someone who has suffered a lot of set-backs despite having worked hard might find it difficult to stomach someone who has been successful without working hard. A man who has had to work hard to control his sexual urges and who has been rigid in his relationships with women might find it difficult to tolerate a man who is more open with women. A person who has suffered a lot from having strict, controlling, authoritarian parents often finds it difficult to cope with those in authority. A young girl who has been sexually abused by her father could find it difficult when she enters into relationships with men who remind her of her father. These people may not be able to analyse or explain the fear and anguish the other people provoke in them; but they experience these feelings nonetheless, and they risk violently rejecting the other person.

Because of my training and experience, I know that I am a strong and effective leader. I can make quick decisions. Some people appreciate and admire this kind of leadership, but I have found that it can make others feel profoundly ill at ease. My presence and power awakens anguish in them of which I am completely unaware. My way of doing things and my lack of listening to people can make them feel small, and confirm for them the feeling that they have no value and nothing to offer. Without our intending it, our being and our attitudes can provoke fear and anguish in others.

Fear of the enemy

When I talk of the enemy, I am not referring to an enemy in war. I am talking about the person in my family, my community, my neighbourhood, my workplace who is close to me, but who provokes fear in me, who seems to prevent me from exercising my particular gifts and from growing towards freedom. This person seems to suffocate and stifle me, to take life from me. If only he or she would disappear from the planet, then I could be free!

For me, Lucien was an enemy. His cries of anguish revealed my own anguish; anguish which seemed to fill my body and make my heart pound until it was difficult to breathe. This anguish in me triggered off feelings of hatred and violence against my will. I never hit poor, weak Lucien, because I was not alone. I was in a milieu which protected me, a milieu which required me to observe certain rules, otherwise I would have been disgraced, judged, made to feel ashamed of myself. I am not saying that, if I had been alone, I would have hit Lucien, but it is clear that the community with all its rules and my need of respect helped me to contain my violence. This painful experience with Lucien helped me feel solidarity with a lot of men and women in prison. When their inner violence was aroused by another person, they were not protected by a milieu which supported humane rules. So their violence led them to hurt or to kill. They were then condemned and humiliated. I was protected. But fundamentally there is no difference between us. There was the same potential to harm a weaker person. When we discover our capacity to hate and harm, it is humiliating. We are not part of an élite, far from it! People who praise us for working with people with handicaps plunge us into even greater confusion because not only are we capable of violence, but we can also be hypocrites hiding behind masks.

At the same time, this humiliation is a good thing. It puts us in touch with our true selves, our poverty. And only the truth can set us free. It is only when we agree to recognise and look at the world of shadows within us that we can begin to travel towards freedom. Then, perhaps, we discover that the enemy is not the other, the stranger, but our own inner demons. The enemy is inside us. The problem is not with the other person; it is in each of us. But how to take the plank out of our own eye before taking the speck from the eye of another? How can we welcome our own brokenness and stop wearing masks?

Expectations which stand in the way of communion

A married woman said to me one day, 'I am living with a man, but he is not the same man as when we married.' She went on, 'In those days, he chased after me, he was full of life and interested in everything I did. Now, he is in a depression.' How hard it is to welcome people just as they are, with all that is beautiful and broken within them! Parents expect a lot of their children. Spouses expect a lot of one another. At l'Arche, the house-leader expects a lot of a new assistant. If we create an image of somebody, and if they do not live up to that image, we feel deceived and tend to reject them. Is that not what happens when a mother gives birth to a little baby boy with a handicap? He is not the baby she dreamed of, so she has difficulty accepting him. The image we have of others, or the image of what we would like them to be, stands in the way of communion. Communion is rooted in reality, not in dreams or illusions. We cannot enter into communion with somebody unless we accept them as they really are.

Each one of us, with our past, our wounds, has difficulties in relationships. We know this. The question is to know how, during the different stages of our lives, and in our journey to wholeness and fullness of life, we can weaken the walls which separate us from each other, and so create communion.

III

THE STAGES OF LIFE

1 Childhood: the time of trust

The child, a person of trust

I do not have any children of my own, and I have
never lived with children, although in certain l'Arche
communities, especially in Haiti, Latin America, Africa
and the Philippines, we have welcomed children, and I
have sometimes been called to follow their development
as human beings. What I have noticed most of all is that,
if they are to grow up happily, they need a secure and loving
environment. When all is said and done, the educational
methods that we are called to exercise with grown-ups at
l'Arche are universal and adaptable to the needs of children
as well as grown-ups.

Claudia was seven years old when she was welcomed into
our community at Tegucigalpa in Honduras. She was blind
and autistic and had been abandoned at a very young age
at the psychiatric hospital 'San Felipe'. In coming to us,
she lost her bearings and became terribly insecure. This
confusion and fear had a shattering effect on her and
left her utterly fragmented. She seemed completely mad,
she screamed during the night, and gnawed her clothes.
Nadine, Regine and Dona Maria welcomed her, along
with Marcia and Lita who also had mental handicaps.
During the months and years that followed, which were
often filled with difficulty and conflict, Claudia was able
to discover that she was respected and loved, and that

there was a place for her. She was able to find security and trust. Today, nearly twenty years later, she is still blind and autistic, but she is peaceful and has an inner calm. She works in the community workshop; she is a serene and, I believe, a happy young woman.

In Claudia's life, as in that of every human being, there is a tension between security and insecurity. Given too much security, we suffocate; we no longer live, we are too comfortable, there is no longer any risk in our lives, we no longer grow. But equally if there is too much insecurity – too much fear and conflict – we do not live. If a child is to develop happily, fear and trauma must be kept to a minimum, there must be a solid and secure base. This base depends on the quality of the relationship between the parents of the young child, and between the child and her parents.

As childhood is a time of growth, it is important for a little boy to be able to learn one thing after another, without contradiction. He cannot cope if one person tells him one thing and another the opposite. He has his own inner logic, which allows him to perceive contradiction, but he does not have the inner strength to deal with it. He needs permanence, routine and coherence. Because he does not have within himself the security to live independently and advance through life, he needs to find it in the trust of another, of his parents, who are there to protect, guide, affirm and love him.

This trust forms the foundations of his personality and it allows him to develop self-assurance and confidence. It gives him stability, strength and a set of beliefs which allow him little by little to welcome and integrate reality, to discover who he is and what are his roots, language, religion, values and family traditions. Knowing who he is, he can then discover who he is called to become.

To develop, this trust requires communication and dialogue. The child speaks and expresses his desires not only through words but also through cries, through his body, and through a whole non-verbal language. Although Claudia did not speak, she nevertheless expressed her desires, anger and suffering through her body and cries. If a child's desires go unattended or are misunderstood, then there will come a time when he will cease to express them. He will close in on himself; within himself he will die. In order to live in trust, a child needs to feel understood. He needs his parents, or the people acting as his parents, to talk and share things with him. The worst thing for a child is to avoid raising certain subjects with him, saying, 'He won't understand.' His parents might, for example, avoid talking with him about the death of his grandmother, or about some traumatic accident, a painful event, about sexuality, and so on. The child then lives in a kind of confusion and fear; his world becomes chaotic and nothing makes any sense. But if his parents get him to talk about some of these questions, and share about them with him, he will then discover that the world and his life are not chaotic; they have a meaning. There is hope.

The child who does not live a relationship of trust is lonely, terribly lonely. He shuts himself off behind walls of fear and pain. He loses contact with reality, slips into a world of dreams and is forced to hide things away and to lie in order to live and survive. The only truth for him is the one he invents.

The child needs to be taught

Claudia needed help not to be closed in on herself, which is the natural tendency of autistic people. Those around her had to struggle with her so that she would not destroy herself but instead discover how beautiful and precious she was, and how she had the capacity to grow. When someone is convinced that they are good for nothing, it takes a lot of time, love and wise relationships for them to discover that in fact the opposite is true.

After many years of living with Nadine, Regine and Dona Maria, Claudia had found a certain peace, and the three assistants had not obliged her to work in the community workshop. It was not until the doctor of the community encouraged them, that they finally decided she had to work with the others. This provoked an enormous crisis. Claudia did not want to leave her private world, where she found comfort. The more a child is closed in on herself, the greater the crisis is going to be when someone urges her to become more open; she needs a lot of help, firmness and encouragement to make this painful transition. She needs to be able to trust the adult who is helping her. A child cannot be forced to grow and become more open through fear. Fear causes people to close up; trust and communion help them to be open. Claudia now finds joy in her work at the workshop, although there are of course still times when she gets angry.

One of the things that destroys trust is conflicting signals. They reveal a lack of coherence in adults: a child is asked to do one thing, but the adults themselves do the opposite. A child normally imitates those adults in whom he has most trust. If there is a discrepancy between what those adults are telling him and how they are living, the child becomes lost and confused. He cannot grow. He is forced to close in on himself.

Several years ago, in the course of making a film, I interviewed a group of fifteen-year-olds who were in difficulty. I raised many questions with them, some easy and some more difficult. Finally I asked, 'What about drugs?' Three of them had had experience of the world of drugs. I got them to talk about their experiences. 'How did your parents react?' I asked them. They replied that their parents had been furious. 'And how did you react to their anger?' One of the teenagers looked at me sharply and said, 'My father is an alcoholic.' I sensed great anger in him. It was as if he were saying to me, 'How dare my father be angry with me when he himself is an alcoholic?' This is what I mean by conflicting signals, saying one thing and doing another. If his father had said, 'My son, do not follow my example. I have inflicted too much suffering on you and your mother,' this would have been *true*, and the dialogue open.

A child sees everything and grasps it all, even if he has not the conceptual powers and the language to articulate it. He is aware, above all, of incoherence and injustice. They shatter his confidence.

One of the difficulties I have encountered in educating and living with people with handicaps is understanding them and walking with them, trying to adapt to their capacities and their true potential. We must not treat them as if they are completely incapable, nor as if they are people more capable than they really are. At the beginning of l'Arche, I fell into this trap through ignorance. I needed to learn to listen to them, to trust their judgment. If we really walk with them, then they know that they can trust others and have confidence in them.

It is difficult for parents to adapt the way they treat their children according to their growing maturity and their changing age. Sometimes parents treat a child of seven as if he were four, or a child of ten as if he were six. The child quickly feels humiliated, because he senses that his parents are not listening to him, do not understand him as he now is and do not trust him. How often parents fail to notice the little gestures of kindness and love that their children offer them. This lack of attention wounds the child.

But when a child feels loved and understood, when he senses that his parents trust him and find pleasure in his company, when they take time to play and laugh and talk with him, then he accepts their remarks and reprimands more easily, and even accepts punishment if it is just and will help him grow. A child needs to know when to stop doing certain things. He needs to understand what is meant by 'law', and to discover that there are limits to bad behaviour. There are things he must not do, such as hit his little brother! It is an important discovery for a child to find that helping his little brother brings joy not only to his little brother, but also to his parents and thus to himself.

When there is no real discipline, the child quickly senses that he has become master of the situation. He cries, he is violent or he breaks his toys until he gets what he wants. He knows what to do in order to get his own way. If a child does not learn that there are limits, it will be very difficult for him later to see others as people, as individuals with their own needs. He will seek always to be in sole charge of the situation so as to get what he wants. This type of situation is particularly difficult and dangerous when the child lives alone with his mother, who is in need of affection because of the absence or the attitude of his father. She risks becoming too emotionally dependent on the child, who will soon discover the power he has over her and his ability to manipulate her.

I have had occasion to speak with parents of adolescents who are taking drugs. They sometimes have great difficulty in being firm, in not allowing themselves to be emotionally blackmailed into giving their son money. They no longer have their own lives, they live only for their son. They want at all cost to stop him from falling into the abyss of despair or from committing suicide. But the son cannot begin to come out of his difficulties unless he respects his parents, sees them as people with their own lives who love him enough to say 'No'.

Bringing up children demands a great deal of perseverance and strength, not a brutal strength, but a gentle one which springs from communion and trust. The child needs to know that he is understood and loved, and that the adult desires his happiness. I was horrified one day when I visited an institution and saw a teacher using an instrument that produced an electric shock on a young girl who was hitting herself. The theory that supports this practice is called 'behaviour modification'; a sensation is transmitted to a person that is either pleasant or unpleasant according to whether it is intended to modify or encourage a certain kind of behaviour. It was hoped that the girl would stop hitting herself because she would discover the link between hitting herself and the unpleasant sensation produced by the electric shock. Obviously, if we love a child, we must encourage her to do good things and discourage her from doing bad, for which we might use one of the universally accepted means of punishment and reward. But in this case, it was clear that the teacher did not love the girl or have any empathy with her, otherwise he would not have been able to hurt her so much. The electric shocks were a kind of torture. Suffering like this cannot heal the girl. She hits herself because she is experiencing anguish which comes from a feeling of being lonely, rejected and guilty. The teacher's action only reinforces this pain. Perhaps the girl will stop hitting herself, but then she will only hide herself away even more behind the walls of a psychosis.

Our experience at l'Arche shows us that these self-destructive acts, which are to a greater or lesser extent caused by fear and self-contempt, cannot be stopped except through years of care, attention and love. This care must come from a group of very united people who are as permanent as possible, and who build up bonds of trust with the suffering person.

Very young children learn principally through imitation. When a child is in communion with his parents and when he trusts them, he seeks to copy them. This is how he learns the language and the gestures essential for life. The parents are his models. The child seems even to detect and copy his parents' faults as well as their good qualities. When we love somebody, we subconsciously seek to adopt their ways.

Teaching through the unity of a couple

Loving a child does not only mean building a relationship of mutual trust. It means helping him to develop, to become responsible, independent, to be himself, free, capable of acting in love – in short, helping him to become fully human. Unhealthy attachment to a child will impede growth towards freedom and independence. It quickly becomes manipulative; communion then becomes possession.

A child needs security, the security of being loved. He needs to feel encouragement from his parents to grow and become responsible. He needs to feel that they trust him. This upbringing is best when the parents love each other and there is tenderness and unity between them; when each of them loves the child not out of an emotional void but out of a heart that is full; when each exerts authority out of his or her own grace and gifts, which complement those of the other. Conflict and division between parents plunge a child into insecurity, because he needs both his father and his mother, and he needs them united. He cannot understand conflict; he may even believe that it is his fault, and blame himself.

In our community in Burkina Faso, we welcomed Karim. His mother had died when he was born, and he had been placed in an orphanage. When he was three, he caught meningitis, and was separated from the other children. The after-effects of the illness were serious; he became unable to speak or to walk, and his intelligence was not able to develop. At the orphanage, he was left on his own in a small room for many years. In his loneliness and anguish, he began to hit his head. When he came to our community, he gradually discovered that he was loved, that he was capable of certain activities. He wanted to live. He stopped hitting his head. But many years later, when there were conflicts and a lack of communication between the assistants, he started again. The lack of unity around him plunged him back into insecurity and anguish.

Faith in the development of the child

One of the difficulties for children is to accept their parents' limitations. At the beginning of a child's life, his parents are everything to him. They are God. All life comes from them. They feed, protect, guide and sustain the child and teach him to speak. Then there are disappointments; hearts are wounded by arguments, fights and tantrums. The child no longer feels understood. He becomes aggressive or depressive. He feels himself either abandoned or suffocated. He may then take his parents off the pedestal on which he has placed them, and hurl them into the pits. Or he may just cut himself off from them emotionally At this moment the child can feel very much alone, and risks condemning himself. Sometimes, he finds support from his brothers and sisters, his school friends, or from an aunt, a godparent or a teacher at school and he simply gets on with living.

What can help the child more than anything to welcome his parents' failings is a faith in God. He can then discover that over and above them and their failings there is a justice, a love, a light and a truth that is universal, and that they are not God. He will then no longer feel judged by the law of his parents or his school or society. Life is not a series of 'Dos' and 'Don'ts'. Life is communion with God hidden in his heart, a God who is good, even if his parents are not always good; a God who forgives, even if his parents do not. This will enable the child to put the absolute where it should be, not in his parents, culture, race or social class; not even in his future or his studies. This implies that he has been introduced to God at an early age through his heart and that he has been able to live communion with God. Then the child discovers God, not as the fruit of his efforts and obedience to the law, but as the source of his own life. This communion with the source of life is sometimes more accessible to a child than to an adult, because he has fewer inner barriers, less pride, less need to prove himself and to be self-satisfied. In short, he lives closer to communion.

Faith allows the child's personal awareness to develop. It allows him to be himself, to discover that it is not just his parents who love him and that, independently of what others think of or want for him, he is precious. It allows him to develop his inner freedom. He has no need to live only in and through the opinions of others.

But in order for the child to live in faith, it is necessary that this should be transmitted as life and spirit. When religion is simply a means of bolstering moral law and order, and not of building communion and love, it becomes oppressive. The child then senses that his parents want him to learn about religion so that he will be good and more obedient to them. Then religion suffocates; it is simply a series of laws to which the child must submit himself. He senses the hypocrisy in this. He cannot cope with a false religion, which serves to favour a controlling authority. But equally, if the child discovers faith as trust in a Person, separate from his parents, his heart becomes open to universal communion.

Parents, or others, cannot transmit faith unless children see that the faith of their parents – or others – makes them 'better' people – humbler, more loving, patient, open and trusting. It should enable them to ask their children for forgiveness when they have been hard or unjust, critical or hypocritical, when they have not put into practice the things that they asked of their children. Children are terribly sensitive to truth. They sense hypocrisy, untruth or injustice. They cannot understand how their parents who claim a certain faith can live the opposite. This is why many children today reject faith as having no human value, as an illusion.

2 Adolescence: the age of searching, generosity, idealism

Adolescence is a tremendously rich time in our life, abounding in opportunities and challenges. It is a time of searching, a time of transition from the values of our family to those we will choose for ourselves. It is a time of instability and sometimes of fear, but it is also a time of hope as vast new horizons open up.

My own adolescence was in some ways displaced by my choosing to join the navy at the age of thirteen. This choice allowed me to leave my family in happy circumstances. It gave me a clear and focused motivation. It gave me a profession and a secure future. It called me to fulfil my physical and human potential, through competition and promotion in what might be called a noble profession. It developed my body and my spirit. But in terms of relationships, I was impoverished through this choice. My energies were so focused on efficiency and success that I had not the time to grow emotionally and to develop my capacity for relationship, outside the friendships which linked me to my fellow officers.

Talking to medical students, or others training for any of the professions, I find that they too are motivated and fired by their studies. Their lives then become structured; their future profession gives them a certain identity. Sometimes, this is detrimental to the development of their capacities for relationship. On the other hand, young people who do not have any particular interests, whether in sport or one of the arts or in their studies, and who have not been able to make a choice concerning their future, can be a bit lost; their energies can be dissipated. They devote most of their attention to their friends and to leisure and cultural activities. But as a result, their cultural experiences and relationships are frequently richer than those of their professionally motivated contemporaries, and thus they can be more open than them.

The suffering common to many adolescents is a lack of self-confidence. Grown-ups seem so certain, strong and competent; adolescents are in need of affirmation. Personally, I was very lucky. When I wanted to join the navy in 1942, in the middle of the war, I was in Canada with my family and the naval college was in England. At that time, the German U-boats were sinking one ship in three as they crossed the Atlantic. So it was not a good time to leave Canada. Of course, I had to talk about my project to my father. He asked me why I wanted to join the navy. I cannot remember exactly what I told him, but I remember his answer. 'I trust you,' he said. 'If this is what you want to do, then you must do it.' I realised much later that his words gave me life. If he had said, 'Wait a bit, in a few years you will be able to enter the training college for the Canadian Navy,' I would have accepted it. But I would have lost faith in my own intuitions. His confidence in me gave me confidence in myself. It helped me to live fully the challenge before me. I did not want to betray his trust.

Friends

Several years ago, twenty-five teenagers aged between fourteen and eighteen, all of them children of l'Arche assistants, gathered for a time of sharing during the holidays. They asked me to talk about the meaning of suffering. I had known a number of their parents before they were married, and felt a bit like their grandfather! None of them was thinking of joining l'Arche later, but they all expressed their joy at living in l'Arche. All had been touched by getting to know people with handicaps. A beautiful friendship had been born between them all. Adolescence is a time of friendship. Friends build a bridge between the warmth and protection of the family, and the new and as yet unchosen earth where they will put down their roots. Friendship is precious. It opens the heart, it gives security, it enables people to take risks. But it is also true that young people can close themselves off behind walls of friendship. They hide themselves from grown-ups; sometimes they hide their despair. They form a separate group.

Teenagers are in the process of leaving their family base. This period of transition is like a journey. They want to find meaning in their lives, they want to find something new, better, more beautiful. They are looking for an ideal to live out.

Ideals

Some young people cannot accept the values either of their parents or of society. These values seem hypocritical. These young people feel betrayed, and sometimes they are angry and rebellious. There seems to be no place for them in a highly organised society. In May 1968 in Europe, young people rebelled against institutions which were too weighty, and an authority which they felt was crushing them. They wanted to show that they too could take decisions, do new things, open new paths.

Young people can be very idealistic; many think they

can change the world. They are beautiful in their desires and their capacity to take risks. This gives them the inspiration and the impetus to do something. Of course, there is an aspect of illusion in their desires, but without them they would do nothing; indeed, nobody else would do anything either!

I am touched today by young people who are in love with noble ideals: ideals of justice for poorer countries, ideals for protecting the environment, spiritual ideals, ideals of peace and of compassion for people who are lonely and in pain. Many are ready to sacrifice their own comfort in order to devote their energies to humanitarian organisations. Others feel disheartened, and shut themselves up in their discouragement. And others want to restore order to a fragmenting society; they engage in rigid and conservative political and religious movements. And there are those who just want to prepare themselves to find a good job and to live like everybody else in a competitive society where money is the most important value.

My experience shows me that there are two kinds of ideal: one which focuses on structures; another which is more directed towards people. The first tends to be militant, seeking to reform social structures and relying on good organisation and a form of propaganda. The other stresses the importance of listening, presence and kindness, changing one heart at a time. Young people who focus their energies on people tend to live closer to human reality than those who seek change through theories, structures and a perfect way of life. The latter can quickly become ideologies which crush people instead of leading them to greater freedom, wisdom and compassion.

In some young people, awareness of the disorder in the world is accentuated by an awareness of their own inner turmoil and darkness. They feel lost, fragile and confused and suffer from a lack of personal identity because of all the conflicts between their own parents. A number of them also feel that their own sexuality is chaotic.

Some time ago, I worked with a group of teachers in a secondary school. Every month we discussed questions affecting adolescents. One day we talked about their confusion faced with sexuality. There is the sexual education they receive in the family milieu, and that which they learn through television; there are their own emotions and the things that they pick up from their school friends. How can they be helped to discover the meaning of human sexuality? I asked the teachers when did they talk about it at school. 'In biology lessons,' they told me. All the teachers admitted that this was not enough, but each of them also confessed that they did not know how to talk about it. It is not surprising that so many people feel confused in this area. What is possible? What is right? What yardsticks are there? What is constructive? What is destructive? The power of attraction towards the opposite sex, the power of desire, the need for more total communion with another leads some people to enter into sexual relations with people with whom they do not have deep bonds of friendship; they are only fleeting, loveless relationships. Sexuality then appears like a wild power, without any human meaning. One woman once said to me, 'When I want to be self-destructive, I enter into a sexual relationship which cannot lead to true relationship.' Another woman who had fallen into delinquency admitted to me, 'When I hate a man, I sleep with him.' In this way, she had him in her power. A tendency not to enter into 'serious' relationships, but to keep relationships on a superficial or merely physical level, can stem from a lack of self-respect. When people do not take themselves seriously, then they will not expect others to take them seriously either.

Human sexuality is a complex reality. Physical union

which is not self-giving leaves people with the impression that all love is in fact deception, separation, and just a game. It thus becomes self-destructive and destructive for others. Pornography, sex shops, sexual abuse, and rape, all show how this power, which is so beautiful when it comes from the heart and gives life and communion, can become life-destroying. AIDS is a disease which creates great confusion; the sperm and blood which are designed to give life instead cause death.

It is not surprising that so many people feel lost before this power of sexuality. Others, however, sense that their sexuality is something sacred; they do not want to give their bodies to just anybody. They feel that human sexuality implies a sacred bond.

One young woman who had lived through a number of experiences with men and with drugs talked to me about a young man who knew her well, 'He loved me for myself.' Some young people make clear distinctions between true and false love. They know when love is true. That is their great strength. They quickly detect hypocrisy and conflicting signals; they sometimes have very acute judgment. Their pain is often that they feel themselves too weak to walk towards the light and towards the ideal that they would have wanted.

Some young people are deeply disturbed by an experience of death, which they encountered at a very early stage. Personally, I did not encounter death during my teenage years. Of course I knew it existed, but I did not live the terrible separation and grief of the death of someone who was close to me. But I have seen the confusion teenagers feel at the death of a school friend – particularly when the death is caused by suicide. Death then seems appalling and unbearable, a manifestation of the chaos of our world. The disorder of the world, their own inner chaos and violence, their consciousness of death and of their own sexual chaos, can lead young people to seek a meaning to all this, to put light into the darkness, order into the disorder, and to live an ideal; or else, as I have said, they fall into a world of disorder and depression. The tendency for many young people is to live more for a beautiful ideal, a theory. They tend to deny reality, or to impose their ideal on reality. It is when they reach maturity that they are able to accept the painful reality of the world and of themselves.

Rules and spiritual guides

Many adolescents, fragile as they are, want to live life to the full. Life surges up in them, they thirst to discover new things, they are filled with curiosity and hope. They want to build a future. They want to take their place in the world. Their own fragility, increased by a feeling of chaos inside and outside of themselves, pushes them towards shaping a new world, sometimes through rigid laws. Because they know that they have neither the strength nor the experience needed to travel alone, they need an intellectual and spiritual formation, a discipline which will help them to formulate and attain their ideals. They need a father or mother figure, a teacher or a guide.

Some of these young people join sects. I was told recently that there are some eight hundred sects in Quebec! Young people, fragile and insecure, feel reassured by rigid rules, by the strong convictions announced by a guru and a group. It is not the less demanding political and religious movements which attract a lot of young people today. Most of them want to do something beautiful with their lives, they are looking for places where they can find meaning in their existence, where they can have a serious intellectual and human formation, and a discipline that will help them to live more fully. They know that if they want to do something good in life, they need to work; to achieve something worthwhile is demanding and requires discipline.

These young people are looking for true witnesses who practise what they preach. They are looking for guides who will bridge the gap between adulthood and life in society and their own lives with all these questions, concerns and hopes – guides who will help them to integrate law into their lives, and help them to discover that law is not something abstract, distant, coming from on high, but something intrinsic to true human life. Laws can sometimes seem rigid, but they are necessary for human beings to blossom and grow, while remaining open to others, just as rules and discipline are necessary to win in sport and study.

Personally, I was helped by Father Thomas Philippe when I left the navy in 1950. I wish that all young people could find a guide like him. Under his influence and guidance, my life was given a new orientation, so that I was more turned towards compassion and truth. I needed a guide and a teacher. I needed a spiritual father, who loved me and gave me confidence in myself, and helped me on my journey of faith.

The adolescent's beauty and poverty

Adolescents are sometimes astonishingly tolerant, sometimes astonishingly intolerant. Many are tolerant, but their tolerance is sometimes the result of a disappointed idealism, or a kind of despair and a mistrust of adults. They do not believe that things can get better. They have not the strength to fight for a better world. Others, on the other hand, are terribly intolerant and idealistic. They criticise everybody. They can be sectarian and hard, even violent towards foreigners and people who are different from them. They can close themselves up in rules and certainties, without opening themselves to others, without listening to them or seeking to understand them.

There is such beauty in adolescence. It is the time of searching and openness, of idealism, generosity and heroism, the time when young people look to the future. But there is also a poverty in adolescence: lack of self-confidence, fear of moving forward or of not succeeding which can lead to closing up. It can become a period of fear and weakness. It is sometimes so difficult to make choices and to earth oneself in a particular spot. The political and social future of our world seems so uncertain. More and more young people are unemployed. And at the same time, young people are presented with so many choices, they are attracted by so many different things. They sometimes want everything, and want it immediately, without having to wait or make an effort. When we make choices, we die a little bit; we renounce other possibilities. This is why they find it difficult to settle. We are in a world that is always changing; everything seems temporary, everything is in a state of flux. Television is constantly presenting new points of view and there are endless new inventions and ways of doing things. What is permanent? Many young people therefore seek to live in the present moment, to live today as powerfully as possible. So how can we help them to have enough self-confidence to make choices, to accept the necessary sacrifices, and to direct themselves down a path of peace and communion, with all the struggle that this implies? How can we help them to live in hope?

3 Adulthood: the time of settling down, fecundity* and responsibility

Settling down

It was in the third stage of my life, at the age of thirty-six, when I became responsible for the people of l'Arche, that I really entered adulthood. The navy had helped to structure my capacities for action and, in some ways, my psychological and physical energies. It had helped me too to make discipline a part of my life (there are plenty of rules in the navy!). The spirituality that I learned and lived through being with Father Thomas, and the philosophical and theological knowledge, shaped and strengthened my mind and spirit. All this prepared me to settle down, to put down my roots, to take on permanent responsibility for others, to find a place where I was able to give others life and to live communion more fully.

At l'Arche I began to understand what adult life really is. L'Arche welcomes many adults with mental handicaps, most of whom find their place fairly quickly after a time spent accepting themselves and discovering their potential and human dignity. At the same time, we welcome many assistants aged between eighteen and thirty for periods

---

* I have maintained the word 'fecundity', even though it is not a common word in everyday English. It is a rich word, signifying fruitfulness and the capacity to give life. (*Translator*)

varying from three months to three years. They are looking for an experience of life and community. They have not yet found a place to put down their roots; they are searching for it. For some people, putting down roots is difficult, because they have so many possibilities before them. They are frightened of choosing too quickly, of losing their independence, or of being disappointed, so they put off making a decision.

In some ways, and with some exceptions, people with mental handicaps do not experience adolescence as such. They do not have a time of searching for ideals. They move quickly from childhood into adulthood and, in the case of some of those with severe handicaps, into old age. This is why some of them seem to have greater maturity than young people of the same age who are searching.

For many people, as for me, the first serious commitment in life is a professional one. This gives a kind of identity. It is chosen during adolescence, and it is confirmed when people start working. Developing our competence helps us to structure our being; this is necessary so that we can earn a living and take our place in society. And here we touch on the tragedy of young men and women who are unemployed. Their emerging identity is put in question. Unemployment is difficult enough for somebody who has already worked for some time, but at least they know that they are capable of working and that they have some value. This is not the case with young adults, who can be completely disoriented when they find no opportunity of proving themselves professionally.

Other young people find structure and stability through their values – moral, social, intellectual and religious. Their stability is strengthened when they become committed to political, social or religious movements. These young people have then made the transition from the faith and values they received from their parents, to a faith and set of values they have claimed as their own. These values inform their choices and the friends they make.

But true human maturity comes when a person takes on a commitment and responsibility to others, a commitment which bonds them to others and which will shape and open their heart and spirit. Most commonly, this commitment takes the form of the bond between a man and a woman who come together to form a family. But there are also commitments to community life, or to social and humanitarian causes inspired by the love of the poor or of people in need.

These choices of permanent commitment imply loss and risk. Loss, because in making a permanent commitment we must give up looking for other experiences, and the freedom to do what we want. Risk, because we do not know how things will evolve. The other person (or other people) might change, fall ill, or be unfaithful, and we ourselves might change. How can we make a permanent choice in a world where everything is changing and evolving so quickly?

At l'Arche, we see how difficult it is for young assistants to commit themselves to the community for life; it is quite a different thing from coming for a few months or a few years. To dare to announce a commitment to a community, a person needs to have been helped to develop her humanity. She needs to have witnessed happy and fruitful examples of permanent commitment, to have found human and spiritual equilibrium in the community, and to have the sense of having grown inwardly, and of having been loved and appreciated.

There comes a moment (and these days it tends to be when people are nearer the age of thirty than twenty) when people feel a kind of call to put down roots and become fruitful, to give life. They are tired of uncertainty and instability, of searching and being on the move; they long to stop. They want to make a permanent commitment to someone who will be their companion on the journey for the rest of their life, or to others in a community life, where people can work together towards an ideal. They know that they are never going to live with an absolutely perfect person; they have begun to accept themselves as they are, and other people likewise. They leave the heights of idealism and dreams to come gradually down to earth. They then become more realistic about the sacrifices they are prepared to make in order to remain faithful, about the difficulties they have in relationships, and about human suffering, through commitment and communion, they discover a new freedom and the joy of giving life.

Fecundity and productivity

In Saint-Exupéry's book, *The Little Prince*, the prince says that we are responsible for the person we have tamed. We become responsible for a heart we have awakened, but even more for the heart of a little child we have brought into the world. Passing on life is one of the deepest human needs. Since the beginning of the world, life has begotten life. Hidden in every creature, flower, fruit, vegetable and tree lie the seeds that produce thousands and thousands of other creatures, flowers, fruits, vegetables or trees. Aristotle says that living things, though themselves mortal, participate in immortality through the permanence of the species and their ability to create new life.

That which is true for every living thing is true in a particular way for human beings. One of the greatest riches human beings can experience is having children. They are the joy of the family. In most parts of the world, a child signifies wealth and security for his or her parents. When the parents are old or ill, the children will look after them. The child is also the future. If there are sexuality and procreation, it is because there is also death. Sexuality and procreation are our response to death. Every human being dies, but we leave behind sons or daughters, similar to ourselves but different. Parents live on in their children, which is why children are either their pride or their shame.

In more affluent societies, however, there is a certain fear of starting a family. Parents are preoccupied with financial problems. Both of them work and are tired; often they cannot obtain suitable housing. Children are seen as a blessing but also as a disturbance and a financial burden. I often wonder whether there is not something else behind the drop in the birth rate in more affluent societies. In l'Arche communities throughout the world there are many married couples. Their salaries are much lower than those of their contemporaries in other walks of life, but they often have three, four or five children. Is this not because in community life in l'Arche they find hope? They are not afraid to bring children into the world.

Human fecundity is not just a biological reality. In order to bring children into the world, a couple must love each other. The foundations for sexual intimacy and procreation are laid through friendship, through a deepening communion, through mutual trust which allows one person to give him or herself to the other. And the child needs their love in order to live and grow without conflict, to become himself and to open himself to others. He needs to be loved, otherwise he will close in on himself. In loving him, the parents communicate life, trust in himself and openness to others; in rejecting him or being too possessive of him, they stifle life. At l'Arche we have seen only too often what happens when a child is deprived of love, or is rejected because of having a handicap.

Fecundity in all human relations

This fecundity of love exists not only in families. It is implied in all human relationships, especially those where one person cares for another. A good teacher is not just somebody who knows her subject and knows how to teach; she loves and appreciates her students, and respects them as individuals. By being respectful, welcoming and loving, she gives them confidence and makes them open to what she has to teach them. This is equally true for priests, doctors, social workers and psychologists, or for those who work with the poor in the slums of Latin America. It is true whenever people meet, and in all activities involving collaboration. We can communicate life and trust to others, but we can also communicate fear. If we enter into a relationship where we dominate, or seek to control others or to prove our superiority, this creates fear and a lack of trust in self. Alternatively, if we remain passive, allowing others to do things as they like, refusing to take responsibility in relationships, this too prevents people from growing to freedom. There is another way: we can enter into a relationship where we affirm the other person, appreciate him, give him confidence in himself and empower him. We help him to discover and exercise his gifts and to develop all that is best in him. A team that works together, a community, or a family, grows when relationships are creative, loving and full of mutual trust.

The vision of l'Arche is precisely this: to help people with handicaps to own their worth and beauty, to help them to have confidence in themselves, with their particular gifts, to grow and do beautiful things, to change the negative images they have of themselves into positive ones. In doing this, we communicate life. Assistants can thus discover their fecundity, and fecundity leads people to become responsible.

Parents are responsible for their children, and this responsibility is demanding. The child has her freedom and, as she grows, expresses it more and more. The parents are responsible for guiding this freedom, not suppressing it. The child is called to grow in freedom – free from fear, free to love, free to know and live the truth. Being a parent is beautiful but demanding.

Fecundity is different from productivity and creativity. There is artistic 'fecundity' which is sometimes magnificent. A work of art, a book, a piece of music, a sculpture, an invention or a painting all first need to be conceived, then spend a certain time in gestation, before an often difficult birth. But the work remains inanimate; it is done, it is beautiful. In contrast, a living thing needs to be fed, loved, educated. We do not sit down and admire it; we cannot put it away in a corner if it is annoying. We are in some way responsible for its growth. Human fecundity springs from communion and finds its completion in another person who is also called to communion. This is why for some people fecundity, or communicating new life, seems frightening. It is less demanding to produce an object which we can put aside when it is no longer wanted, than to be responsible for the life of a child or another person. In becoming responsible, we become more human, we grow in maturity and we open ourselves to others.

A work of art, like all human works, can favour relationships or render them more difficult. In this way, it participates in fecundity. There are paintings, icons, types of music, plays, songs and poems which open the heart to communion. They are created out of an experience of communion and directed towards communion. In the same way, architecture or the way a house is furnished can be either conducive or not conducive to intimacy and human well-being.

Adolescents live the risk of searching. Adults live the risk of love and fecundity. Often, the person for whom we are responsible leads us where we do not want to go. Is this not the case with so many parents who have been opened up and changed by their children?

Authority and responsibility

Human maturity is the capacity to exercise authority and to assume responsibility for others. An adolescent searches for a place to put down roots. An adult puts down roots in a particular place and can then bear fruit. Adults become responsible for others: responsible for a wife or husband, for children, friends and workmates; responsible for those they have helped, or in whom they have awakened life. And responsibility involves exercising authority.

In our age, there is a great fear of authority and responsibility. A person who exercises authority is often seen as one who stifles others' freedom in order to manifest power and obtain what he or she wants. This may sound like a caricature, but in reality many people do not know how to exercise authority. They exercise it like an angry sergeant major, by shouting.

At l'Arche, I have discovered two kinds of authority: an authority which imposes, dominates and controls; and an authority which accompanies, listens, liberates, empowers, gives people confidence in themselves and calls them to be aware of their responsibilities. The person who exercises authority in the first way is convinced that he is right. He has a sense of duty, and he wishes to teach others human, religious and moral truths. The subordinate person, meanwhile, has nothing to say; he must listen, learn and obey. There is no discussion. The person who exercises this kind of authority may well have a sense of the truth. He is not necessarily looking for glory, and he may not want to crush others. But he does not know how to walk with another on his journey; he does not really respect him. He does not listen to him. He tends, in spite of himself, to look down on him and treat him as inferior.

This kind of firm authority is necessary in times of crisis. When there is a fire, it is essential to act quickly and efficiently. A child must know that there are things he or she must not do. We must know how to be firm and say 'No!' when faced with a person who treats people with handicaps contemptuously and abusively. It is important to correct injustice. It is vital to stop a young person from allowing him or herself to slide into drugs. In the Gospel, we are told that Jesus made a whip from cords and drove the animals out of the temple; he upset the tables and the money-changers' money. He also shouted against the pharisees who put heavy burdens on the shoulders of the poor and weak. We must stop crime and oppression. Then, certainly, we must resume discussion, seek to understand, to be reunited at a deep level with those who have done wrong and try to enable them to change and evolve more humanly, to take responsibility for their lives and the lives of others. Similarly, in teaching, there are scientific and human truths which we must sometimes teach clearly in order to prevent people falling into error and confusion.

This force of authority must be used above all against certain strong people who abuse their power and their cleverness to crush the small and innocent, who cannot defend themselves. Jesus said that the strong person who leads astray a little one by sullying his love and innocence, deserves to be thrown into the sea with a huge boulder round his neck. Strong words!

The authority which listens and helps people to assume their responsibilities and to have confidence in themselves is founded on communion. Parents who play with their children, listen to them, love them, and who are good and just, build confidence. They exercise authority with trust so that their children can live, be free and grow towards maturity. And the children respond to the trust placed in them. This kind of authority does not impose the truth on people, but helps them to discover it. It does not make people learn rules, but helps them to understand the meaning and the 'why' of the rules. This requires steady support and takes time, because it is a matter of meeting other people where they are, until little by little, according to their capacity and their inner rhythm, they make the truth a part of their life. This kind of authority helps others to have confidence in themselves and in their inner journey, and to become responsible.

Authority of a kind which accompanies and walks with people sometimes gives way to a third kind of authority, silent, loving and hidden – an authority which does nothing, which waits, builds trust, and sometimes watches night and day in anguish. There comes a point, for example, when a father knows that it is no longer fitting for him to advise his son; he is grown up now and must assume responsibility for himself, even if he makes mistakes. It is the same for the mother of a daughter addicted to drugs, on the road to death. She has expressed her anguish, but communication has broken down and communion is damaged. The daughter has gone. The mother waits, her heart pierced with suffering. The daughter has her freedom. The mother cannot control her. Perhaps one day she may hit rock bottom and come back. There will be nothing left for her but to die or to climb back up. And the mother keeps her trust in life and sometimes in God. In this case, authority looks like weakness and poverty. There is nothing more she can do. She waits for her child to return; she waits for communion. Perhaps, through her littleness and her tears, her broken heart, she draws her daughter towards her, she who was not able to draw her through strength and wisdom.

I know certain people who cannot assume active and direct responsibility for others. This is not their mission – perhaps sometimes because of their fragility. On the other hand, they assume indirect responsibility for many people through their compassion, through offering their lives, through their prayers. Their role is very hidden, as in the third form of authority. Through their poverty and their love, they play an important role in a community and in the world.

A good and kind father confided to a friend, 'I had got into the habit of telling my teenage son exactly what he should do. But my relationship with him deteriorated. Then I decided to change my attitude and listen to him. Since then our relationship has really improved. Trust has been re-established.' This is an example of two kinds of authority.

In the army, authority is exercised above all by giving orders, even though dialogue is often used. At l'Arche, we seek instead to exercise authority through accompanying others and helping them to become responsible, but at other moments we too have to give orders.

There are many symbols of a just and good authority. The *gardener* who waters and nourishes the plants does not manufacture nor control life; she helps it to grow. The *good shepherd* knows each lamb by name and has a special relationship with each; he leads his flock and risks his life to defend his lambs from the wolves. The *rock* on which we can lean provides support. The *source of water* which washes and refreshes signifies forgiveness which is at the heart of all real authority.

Some assistants at l'Arche have had bad experiences of authority as children: perhaps their father was not around, or perhaps he was very authoritarian and stifled their freedom. So many people have never experienced the kind of authority which helps others to get back on their feet again, to recover confidence in themselves, to become freer. In order to exercise properly the authority which implies a real listening and understanding of others, we need time, experience and support. We must either have received or experienced this kind of authority. To become truly responsible, we must have lived with a person who was truly responsible. To know how to command, we must know how to obey. The exercise of authority demands humility. Authority then becomes a service which transcends the person. It is a risk, because we cannot always be sure of helping another person and of communicating life.

Those who have suffered a crushing authority which dominates and controls often go on to reject all forms of authority. Authority is then regarded as something bad because it has tended to suppress freedom. These people often refuse to assume responsibility, they run away from it, or else they too tend to exercise authority harshly. They cannot stand confrontation coming 'from below', just as they cannot stand authority coming 'from above'.

Anarchy quickly engenders dictatorship. Where there is a lack of authority, a powerful authority often moves in. This makes people feel secure, but then it can become controlling and dominant. It is not easy to find a happy medium – an authority which listens, understands, is sensitive and seeks to help others to grow.

In Latin cultures, there is a tendency to elaborate a theory, an ideal, and then to impose it. Reality has to be modelled, changed and transformed according to a theory or an ideal. The ideal is like the prototype, like the architect's plan. Anglo-Saxon cultures, on the other hand, are more pragmatic. They deal with, and in, reality, but often they lack vision; they do not always know where they are going or have a long-term plan. True authority does not seek to impose an ideal, but rather to guide reality towards an attainable and possible end. It does not impose, it guides.

Working for justice

If fecundity and responsibility unfold and grow within families, then the same will happen in society. Our families prepare us to be good citizens. When human beings put down roots and settle in a particular place, and as they learn to become responsible within the family, so they learn to become responsible in society. As adults we are no longer surrounded simply by friends, as we were as adolescents. We discover a world full of stark contrasts, where there is suffering, inequality and injustice, and where authority is sometimes exercised well and sometimes less so, a world in which we too must take our place. There is a parish council, there is the local government which makes more or less just decisions; in industry there are unions to deal with injustice. At all levels in the worlds of work and of politics, we are all called to take our place and to work for justice. There are things that need to be said about the school where our children are, about the development of the town or village and the local community, about sorting out human problems so that people can grow towards greater wholeness and come together in friendship and listen to each other. If we see the Gospel as good news which gives life and hope, it is important that we become involved in the parish, helping to do things like making the liturgy more lively. When we settle in a particular area or job, we discover our responsibilities *vis-à-vis* other colleagues, society and the organisation of which we are a part. If we want life and society to be better organised, then we must do something about it. We must take our place within its structures and not leave others to take all the decisions. We must assume our responsibilities as citizens, members of a church, workers in industry, according to our abilities and capacity for action. We must take our place in the creation of just laws, which permit human beings to live more humanly. Are we not all responsible, each according to his or her gifts and mission, for the creation of a better society where human beings can live in peace and trust with one another; where each person can grow in humanity, and where each feels respected and finds what he or she needs to communicate, live and grow? We must struggle on behalf of all that helps the growth and true freedom of society, and against all that dehumanises, stifles, enslaves. Sometimes struggling in this way leads to rejection or imprisonment, even to torture or death. But is it not in such giving that our lives bear fruit?

The exercise of authority: a school of maturity

Many people find exercising authority painful. I have seen this at l'Arche. When someone has been an assistant in a house for one or two years, we ask them to become the leader in a house where there are perhaps five people with handicaps and three or four assistants. To begin with, they feel a certain joy in being called to responsibility; they feel loved, appreciated and affirmed by those who have called them to this responsibility. This helps and strengthens them. They discover that they have gifts of leadership, but gradually they also discover that assuming responsibility has its painful aspects. Some of the other assistants contest their authority, others lack enthusiasm. The person is obliged to remind them of the rules, to urge them out of their lethargy. These coercive aspects of authority are tiring. In taking on new responsibility, the person wanted to be loved; she did not want conflict. She discovers within herself her own anger and depression. She gets fed up and would like to give up; she wants to escape the loneliness that comes with responsibility. It is sometimes easier to let everybody do what they like and to say nothing. Parents live through the same thing with their children. After they have tried to use force and threats of punishment to make their teenage son or daughter obey their rules, they give up because they cannot face further conflict. Even less can they face their own anger and violence. So they let their children do what they like.

Personally, I learned a lot while I was responsible for l'Arche. It brought me suffering; I did not like opposition and situations of conflict; but at the same time I found great joy in exercising responsibility and in discovering that through it I could give others life. Over the years, my way of exercising authority has evolved. At first, I exercised it in the way that I had done in the navy; I knew what was right, others did not. I was in charge and the others had to do what I demanded of them. It was simple. This way of organising things suited people who were insecure and needed a strong person in charge. But to some who were older and more thoughtful, and who had a clearer vision of the community, it was wounding. I was not aware of how I hurt some people, by being strong and taking quick decisions without allowing them to formulate their own vision and, if necessary, to contradict me.

In those days, I used to find it unsettling when members of the community stood against me in some way. As I had invested myself completely in the community, I interpreted any disagreement as hostility toward me. When people opposed some of my decisions, I assumed that they were in fact opposing me. I sometimes felt anger and a kind of inner violence welling up in me. I could control these and hide them, but they were there nonetheless, signs of my vulnerability. It then became tempting to start thinking of the members of the community in terms of friends and enemies. It was some time before I had enough inner peace and was able to stand back and appreciate that it was important to have different people in the community, to respect their differences and to see their worth. I was not the only one with good ideas and a vision for the community; these had to come from all of us!

There were times when I tended to get completely caught up in things that needed to be done. I hid myself behind over-activity, rules or discipline. Through weariness, fear or pride, I would cut myself off from people. When we listen to people, and discuss things with them, we become more vulnerable; errors, faults and incompetence become more obvious. So it is tempting to hide ourselves behind a clear, predetermined programme. I learned little by little to become vulnerable enough to allow myself to be changed by reality, and by the ideas of others.

I see the danger for some community leaders in l'Arche of becoming closed up in an administrative role and hiding themselves behind rules. Maintaining principles becomes more important than people. This way of exercising authority involves fewer risks, at least in the short term. Exercising responsibility over people with whom we are in communion is complex and 'dangerous'. We must be ready to listen to them, talk with them, allow ourselves to be changed by them. The danger for people in politics or in the Church, or for anyone in a position of authority, is that they lose contact with people and close themselves up in ideas or programmes which they want to impose on others.

The experiences of many assistants at l'Arche shows me that exercising responsibility as a service to others is an important part of the journey towards maturity. But it is never easy. Finding the right balance between turning our back on difficult situations and imposing our will and dominating, implies having sufficient distance to be able to see more clearly the reality of what is happening. This means developing an inner strength and peace, and developing the capacity to listen and talk and co-operate with others for a common good which is greater than any of us. These qualities are not confined to certain people. They are necessary in the exercise of all forms of authority, beginning with parental authority. Developing them demands time and help from friends and people who can accompany us and in whom we can confide.

Adulthood: the discovery of faults and guilt

If children can become paralysed by fear, and teenagers by a lack of hope and self-confidence, adults are sometimes paralysed – more or less consciously – by guilt which leads them to shut themselves off from others and prevents them from giving life and being responsible.

We have already talked about psychological guilt (or shame), the feeling that is imprinted on the heart of a child as a result of a rejection that has made him believe that he is bad and incapable of pleasing others. This broken self-image is at the root of all the lack of self-confidence that is found in adults, all the fears which prevent people from talking, from assuming responsibility for others. It pushes some to try to compensate by demonstrating their power, by proving through their activities that they are admirable.

There is also moral guilt, experienced above all by adults who accept responsibility for other people. A teenager is almost bound to cause his parents pain. He has to establish his identity, to learn to say 'No!', and to break away from them. On the other hand, the adult who puts down roots in a family makes a commitment to a husband or wife. He or she makes a vow of love and takes on responsibility for children. Maturity involves responsibility and fecundity, but these imply choices, fidelity and perseverance. Maturity requires efforts to remain patient, to listen to another, and to become interested in their interests, in order not to become imprisoned in a state of egoism where we see ourselves as the centre of everything.

It is easy to allow ourselves to be seduced by selfishness and superficial needs, by a desire to increase our power, influence and salary, to the detriment of communion, community and our responsibilities as human beings. We can be unfaithful to our word and responsibilities. We can be bad spouses, bad fathers, bad mothers, cutting ourselves off from loving relationships. We can despise the weak and the poor, refuse to listen to their cry, close ourselves up in wealth and possessions and squander money on superficial things. We can allow ourselves to be drawn into corruption and lies. We can torture, oppress and kill; we can abuse children. This is where moral guilt is born.

It is always possible to find psychological excuses for unfaithfulness, excuses based on past wounds. But the fact remains that through our actions or indifference, we hurt people and fail to come to their aid and to assume human responsibility. We do not live in solidarity with others. Instead of being fruitful and giving life, we spread death.

Guilt is like a spear embedded in our consciousness; it is unbearable. This is why people suffering from guilt escape into different forms of addiction: theories, illusions, hyperactivity or an endless pursuit of pleasure. In order to escape their guilt, they find a thousand ways of forgetting and of justifying themselves, while condemning and judging others. Their guilt expresses itself in attacks on society, the Church, people in authority, parents. Everybody else is at fault. They then live a kind of lie, frightened of being discovered. This cuts them off from the source of their being and prevents clarity and openness in relationships. If guilt is painful, it is also beneficial. In some people the throbbing pain of guilt calls them to change, to seek the truth, to repair past faults and to ask forgiveness.

Guilt undoubtedly has psychological foundations. Psychological guilt is at the root of moral guilt. When a child has not been loved and has been accused of being bad, she can become so convinced that she is bad that she automatically does 'bad' things. If she feels convinced that she has hurt her parents, she risks hurting others. It is only when a child has had an experience of being loved, of her own goodness, beauty and hidden light, that she can choose to love and give life to others.

Moral guilt reinforces psychological guilt. A person becomes increasingly convinced that she is bad and that there is no hope for her. Her self-image becomes more and more broken, and this drives her to do things which destroy life.

An adolescent lives in hope, searching for a place where he can put down roots. As an adult he comes back down to earth when he settles down with others. But in doing this, he is soon forced to face all his difficulties in relationships, his fears and blockages. He then experiences guilt. He is pretty well obliged to recognise all that is broken within him. How can he be helped to become free from all this brokenness and guilt, so that he can live with responsibility and fecundity in a realistic and humble way?

4 Old age: the time of serenity and loss

Old age

I have officially moved into retirement. Born in 1928, I am sixty-eight as I write this. I still feel full of energy, but at the same time I know that my official duties in l'Arche are easing off. It is the beginning of old age, the last stage of my life.

Since 1980 I have ceased to be the person with overall responsibility for the community of l'Arche. Gradually, I have withdrawn from having specific responsibilities within the community. This change has brought me both relief and grief. Relief, because being responsible for a community as important as the one in Trosly-Breuil is an onerous task. There are so many things to do. It is not a question simply of making a complicated organisation work, but also of being responsible for a community, for individuals. I do not like conflict. I have a tendency to take criticism too personally. But people in positions of responsibility need to know how to resolve conflict and to welcome criticism. So giving up responsibility was a real relief. But it also caused me grief. When you are used to taking decisions, it is difficult when suddenly you have nothing more to do. When for sixteen years lots of people have consulted you on matters concerning the community, or come to ask your advice, it is painful to accept that they now consult someone else. It is hard to lose control over people and situations.

Old age can be a happy time. Some people get involved in

lots of new interests; others feel finally free from duties. Elderly people no longer need to prove themselves. They can do all the things they have not had time to do before: open their hearts to others and listen to them, because they no longer have any reason to be defensive. They can live communion and take time to celebrate and pray. But it takes time to adjust to being no longer involved in bigger, more competitive activities through which they can prove their worth and importance. Without them, there is a vacuum, a feeling of death, and of rejection. Sometimes I felt terrible anger welling up in me because I felt I had been pushed aside, not fully recognised or valued. Old age is a journey towards communion, towards accepting weakness. Old people rediscover what they lost as children when they began to pursue power and success in order to establish an identity. They rediscover the beauty and simplicity of daily life. But if day-to-day communion is to fill the vacuum, they need to know how to pass through difficult moments. I have had to pass through them. I have had to learn to live through grief and loss.

Bereavement

A bereavement is the loss of someone or something vital, who or which fills our spirit and heart, brings us alive, and calls forth our energies. This loss leaves an inner emptiness; our energies are no longer called forth. We feel disoriented and confused. The energy is still there, it is part of us, but we no longer have anything to focus it on. Emptiness or boredom turns into anguish. If we are to welcome the great bereavements of old age and death, we need to pass through stages, to have learnt to welcome all the little bereavements which begin early on in life and continue to occur throughout.

At l'Arche, I live with men and women who have lost

before having ever gained. They have not enjoyed good health; many have not had families who welcomed them with love, respect and tenderness. They have experienced emptiness in their lives without having ever known fullness. Many have been separated from their parents and placed in institutions or psychiatric hospitals at an early age. Some of them have even refused to grow and to live; they are imprisoned in sadness and feelings of death. Life has not flowed in them.

Losing things or people that are dear to us is something that happens to all of us at every stage of our lives. For a tiny child, being born means losing the security of her mother's womb; it is a moment of anguish. With the loss of security, she succumbs to anguish, but life urges her forward and she searches for another kind of security. A girl loses a special place as the only child in the family when a little brother or sister is born. She is no longer the centre of attention; there is someone else. This can plunge her into anguish, anger, rebellion, but at the same time it can become a moment of growth, helping her to progress towards greater autonomy.

Not long ago, I had a letter from a mother who told me about her twenty-five-year-old daughter who had started to behave very aggressively towards her. She could not understand this change of behaviour. The daughter, with the help of a therapist, was becoming aware of an immense inner anger towards her mother, an anger that began when, at the age of two, she was sent to stay with her aunt while her mother gave birth to a second child. She had lost her mother without understanding why. She believed she had been abandoned. This anger hidden in her for twenty-three years suddenly erupted in her consciousness. Loss often provokes anger. It is important to free ourselves by expressing in words what we have never dared to express, what has remained locked up in the unconscious. In this way we can let go of grief and accept loss, because we can talk about it and understand what has happened and, if necessary, forgive the person concerned.

One of my friends was finishing a doctorate in philosophy. He was a brilliant man. He had already been offered an important teaching post in a university. His future was assured. Then he fell ill and was found to have a brain tumour. After a difficult operation, he could no longer read. For two years he lived in a state of confusion, rebellion and anger. It seemed to him that his whole life had collapsed; he was completely disoriented. Then, gradually, he began to discover the joy of relationships and of listening to others. After two years, he was able to say to a friend, 'I can now accept all that has happened. Before, I lived for books and ideas. Now that I can no longer read, I live with and for people, and I am happy.' He had oriented his life towards listening to and helping people in difficulty. He had said goodbye to philosophy.

I am often in contact with mothers who have been bereaved of the child of their dreams, a child in good health. When they discover that their child has a serious mental handicap, their inner world collapses. Giving birth to a child with a severe handicap seems something terrible and incomprehensible. Immediately, the parents feel guilty and start asking questions, 'What have I done wrong to have a child like this?' This is the cry, often not articulated, of many parents. It takes time for them to welcome reality, not to be submerged in disappointment and anger. We all live with plans for ourselves, our children and our friends. If life does not work out according to our plans, then depression, anger, rebellion, sadness and accusations set in.

For those who have thrown themselves into an ideal, there is frequently a time of disappointment, a time when they have to face reality as it is. For some, marriage begins by seeming like bliss, a perpetual honeymoon where two people are in love with each other for ever and ever. Then comes the time when they become aware of the other's limitations, and of their own. They even become aware of a poverty of love, which can turn into anger and hatred. The greater their dreams, the harder it is when they hit reality.

Some people who devote their lives to movements based on high ideals live through a similar disappointment. They might, for example, have devoted themselves to a political ideal. So many men and women saw in Communism an ideal vision for humanity, but then they were disappointed when they discovered all the lies, cover-ups and corruption. Similarly, there have been people disappointed by religious communities, by the Church and by l'Arche. They have wanted to devote their lives completely to a community. Then they have discovered the disappointing reality: members of the community closed in on themselves and jealously guarding their privileges, difficult characters, internal conflicts, badly exercised authority. Loss of an ideal can lead to confusion and anger. It is as if someone has deceived us by parading before us an ideal that is in fact nothing but an illusion. Yet the love of an ideal is necessary. It gives us the impetus to do something and to work for change and reform. But the return to reality is necessary and painful.

One of the greatest kinds of suffering I have encountered is that of young women who want to marry, but for whom no partner has turned up. One girl admitted to me that she could never be happy if she did not get married. She said that if nobody chose her, then she would feel as if she did not really exist. I tried to point out that marriage did not always bring happiness, that many marriages break down or become filled with conflict, that children often cause difficulties. But nothing seemed to free her. Reasoning does not help people to overcome grief. They need something else: the discovery of another joy, another fullness despite, or even because of, the grief. You cannot help a mother to accept her child with a handicap by telling her that he is beautiful, that there are things he will be able to do and gifts he will develop. She needs to have a new experience through which her 'grief will turn into gladness'. This was the promise that God made to Jeremiah: 'I shall turn their grief into gladness, comfort them, and give them joy after sorrow' (Jer. 31:13). After experiencing community life, and having other more inner experiences, the young woman who was so desperately longing for marriage began to discover that happiness is not necessarily linked to the love of a man. Happiness could be found within herself. It was a question of changing her attitude with regard to reality and events. The experience of God helped her to discover who she was, that her life was beautiful, that she had a unique value which could blossom, that the love and fruitfulness she was looking for were possible in other forms.

A l'Arche assistant once admitted to me that the great wound of his life was that his father despised him. He was very different from his brothers, who had all been successful in business and had good jobs. He had never been a success. He suffered terribly from his father's scorn. It is terribly painful for a son not to live up to the expectations of his parents. He had therefore ended up at l'Arche. He had not positively chosen to be there; he just could not think what else to do with his life. Little by little, he discovered the strength of community life, the human and Christian vision of l'Arche. He discovered that there were things he could do, that he was capable of assuming responsibility. He discovered faith and the love of Jesus. He was then able to recognise that, while it looked from the outside as if his brothers had been successful, a dimension of joy and faith, and a deep motivation, were perhaps missing in their lives. His grief changed into gladness and this became stronger as his ageing father began to admire his way of life.

The grief of old age begins in the middle of adult life. There is a kind of grief people suffer at around the age of forty which is in fact the grief of adolescence prolonged in adult life. Life is no longer before us, it is behind. We discover that we cannot dream as we did before. Choices have been made, and the opportunities for change and for a new life have narrowed considerably. And perhaps we are faced with all sorts of unexpected difficulties at home or at work. Then, sometimes, we find ourselves working with younger people who are more able, and who are being promoted faster. All this is a sign of approaching old age. It takes time to find the rhythm of life and the spiritual nourishment necessary to change our attitude and to welcome reality with serenity. Sometimes the refusal to accept the transition into middle age leads men and women to relive their adolescence or to live an adolescence which they have never lived. They then sometimes take new emotional risks by entering into affairs which are often bound to turn out unhappily. The grief experienced in moving into our forties is different for a woman than a man. The menopause brings a definite end to a part of her life; it is no longer possible for her to have children. This often leads to a real feeling of loss.

One of the greatest griefs of life is the loss of honour, the experience of being despised, seen as someone who has betrayed a cause. This was the immense suffering of Jesus. After all he had achieved, the crowd, which had followed him and seen him as the prophet who was going to bring liberation to a humiliated and crushed Jewish people, then rejected him. He was misunderstood and abandoned by his friends. The crowd that on Palm Sunday had cried out, 'Hosanna, Hosanna, Son of David, King of Israel!', on Good Friday cried, 'Crucify him, Crucify him!', implying, 'He has deceived us'. It is a terrible suffering to be abandoned by friends who have lost confidence in us. Fear of this is the most profound kind of panic that I can experience. From some points of view, l'Arche can be seen as a success for me, although I am convinced that it is not my work but the work of God. There is a kind of peace and joy in knowing that I am supported and loved by so many friends, brothers and sisters, that I have been chosen by God to live the reality of l'Arche, that I have had a full and fruitful life. To lose all this, to lose the security, friendship and intimacy of brothers and sisters, to feel devalued, rejected and condemned would seem to me the ultimate bereavement. If I think of being stripped bare in this way, panic wells up in me. And yet the promise of God remains, 'I will turn their grief into gladness.'

The more we are taken up with something, with a project, with friendship and honour, with an ideal of life which stimulates and attracts us, the harder the fall is when this reality collapses. Suddenly, we find ourselves without life, and without desire or hope. This is depression, a feeling of death. We are lost and confused. It takes time for energy to come back, for new plans to form, for our appetite for life to be restored.

Psychologists, and above all those who have accompanied people suffering from terminal cancer, have described the different stages towards acceptance of this reality, but these stages are the same in all forms of grief. First, there is a refusal to believe. The patient rushes to another doctor. But there comes a time when he can no longer escape the reality. Then everything seems to collapse, and there is rebellion, anger with reality, anger with God, anger with others. He closes himself up in his anger, asking, 'Why me?' But we cannot remain in a state of rebellion, we look for ways out. We can try to change reality by negotiating with God over our destiny, 'If I say this prayer or make this pilgrimage, if I stop smoking, if . . . , if . . . , if . . .' But nothing alters the reality, and so we sink into depression and sadness. We remain imprisoned in ourselves until the day comes when something happens. A ray of light enters the heart, there is an encounter, and we begin to welcome reality, to accept the situation as it is. We discover that our task is not to shape reality, but to accept and discover within it a light, a new love, a presence. Many transitions that imply grief can become easier if we prepare for them and choose them rather than allowing ourselves to become subject to them. We can prepare ourselves for the transition into middle age or retirement, even the transition into death.

Living my own grief

I have myself passed through times of grief, but the emptiness or vacuum or inner pain that I have experienced have never been very long because my energies have never been fixed on only one thing. Bringing to birth and guiding the community was never my only occupation. I have always kept up my intellectual interests. And even though I was leader of the community, I also lived the joys of communion with members of my community and with my friends outside the community. Since 1968 I have given retreats, announced the Gospel, the good news of Jesus, not only to the communities of l'Arche and Faith and Light, but also to other people who wanted to allow the light of Jesus into their lives, to free themselves from their selfishness and the fears that paralysed them, to allow their faith to inspire their lives. And I have always kept up a life of prayer and communion with

Jesus. Now, I feel happy that my life is less taken up with plans and things to do. I have less need to prove myself. I am happy to let others organise and control.

But I know there will be other forms of grief in the future, when I have less energy, when I fall ill, when I can no longer help people with advice, friendship and support; when, on the contrary, I need others to help me because I have become weak. Shedding these things is necessary in order for me to come closer to the reality of my being, because I am still attached to many things, to a certain need to be recognised and respected. There are still systems of defence around my heart; there are still walls that must fall so that I can be more closely in contact with the source of my being; so that I may become, in the deepest sense, who I really am. In order to live communion with God in the fullest sense, we must fall down into the depths of the pit, so that we can rise up again more alive.

All these types of grief enable us to discover that we human beings really need to live through the different stages of life in order to become fully ourselves. We need the trust of childhood, the boldness and hope of adolescence, the stability, fecundity and responsibility of adulthood – even if in each of these stages, motivation is mixed and ambivalent. Obviously, in the beautiful things that we do and in our struggles for justice, there is always a certain self-seeking and a need to prove ourselves, but these acts also have their own beauty and truth. They are necessary for the fulfilment of our being. Grief is necessary too. It is like a pruning, a pruning to help us return to what really matters and to communion. We then no longer live in a world of dreams or by escaping into the future, and we are not dependent any more on what others think of us and on their admiration. There comes a time when we can no longer hide. We simply meet God in our poverty, and he calls us to enter into communion with him.

The end of life

In the following chapters, we will see how a true experience of God, revealed to us in our poverty, is the most profound way to cope with grief, to overcome life's frustrations and to live in reality. One of the most dangerous things human beings can do is to remain closed and focused on themselves and their plans, clinging to their reputation and glory, living in an imaginary world as if they were eternal, or as if they were God. Human life is a journey home, a journey towards becoming what we really are, towards finding our deepest identity and gradually opening ourselves to others. It is a question of being, and being open. Grief comes as we are cut off from the things that we enjoyed and gave us life, yet which kept us away from what is deepest in us. But that does not mean that as we are thus pruned we will necessarily open up. Grief and loss can bring rebellion and depression. Pruning is painful. We can close up even more on ourselves. But it is also through grief and emptiness that renewal can come about as we become more open to communion with our universe, with others and with God.

The last stage of life is filled with bereavements and loss which prepare us for death; strength diminishes, health declines, memory weakens. Old people feel less able to face conflict and they lose their friends. The end of life resembles the beginning; old people who are incontinent, who need to be fed, washed and dressed, who no longer communicate so much through words as through the eyes, touch and smiles, are like little children. We are conceived and born for communion with our mothers and fathers. When we are old or sick, we become weak and small again, and then we rediscover the gift of communion.

Old age and dying

Whatever turns life takes, old age remains a time of suffering. Some old people grow more gentle and kind, they live communion and become more human. Some grandparents are surrounded by their children and their grandchildren. But today, in our affluent countries, there are more and more grandparents who cannot stay with their children. They feel lonely and abandoned. So today, many old people are filled with sadness and inner emptiness. Many have been widowed, and live with the constant pain of having lost their lifelong companion. Many spend their time in front of the television, because it helps to kill time, or else they focus all their attention on one person, becoming desperately possessive of them and refusing them their freedom. They live in boredom, depression and fear. Many have had to retire to old people's homes, cut off from the world, from young people, from their friends and from the environment they are familiar with, without any cultural, emotional or spiritual input. Many old people suffer intensely. They feel useless, unwanted and a burden to their children. They lack the strength, energy and interest to read. They wait for others to do things for them. It takes very little to make them panic. All the feelings of broken communion that we have already described in the child resurface in their consciousness: feelings of guilt, worthlessness, depression and rebellion.

Lately, I had the privilege of being close to two old people, my mother and Father Thomas. Both of them were in many ways full of peace and serenity, welcoming reality and other people, and above all those who were distressed or lonely. But how both of them suffered, and how they were sometimes filled with anguish during the last months and years of their lives! The lack of energy, the consciousness of their limitations, the lack of sensitivity in people close to them, a world which seemed to pass them by or leave them feeling lonely, lost and helpless, sometimes sent them into paroxysms of anguish and inner suffering, in which nobody could really reach them. What can we say about this final anguish, this terrible feeling of being abandoned and unwanted, of dying an inner death? Perhaps the fuller a life has been with light, clarity, friends and success, the more terrible the emptiness and anguish of old age seem.

I have begun to feel these pangs of anguish: when the nights are long and I cannot sleep; when I do not have the energy to think, pray or read; when I feel jumpy and on edge; when my imagination becomes wild, mad and out of control; when feelings of fear, panic and guilt rise up. The night sometimes seems so long, and the dawn so far away! Of course, I can still try to offer up to God all the pain, but that offering seems so little and inadequate. Faith is so delicate a thread, but it permits me to live in hope.

Death

In the communities of l'Arche, we have lived through many deaths. There are deaths that are gentle and beautiful, like those of Agnes, René and Jacqueline. They became gradually weaker, surrounded by their friends. The people living in their houses regularly shared their thoughts about their friend who was dying, and prayed for them. Then, one day, the little, fragile flame of life went out.

There are deaths which are sadder and more difficult, when death comes unexpectedly, like a thief in the night, and people die alone in hospital. Friends are not able to surround them and say goodbye to them.

Then there have been violent, terrible, shocking deaths; deaths of young and beautiful assistants, full of life, killed in car accidents. These deaths leave a void, and give rise to anguish and fear. They oblige people to face their own death: 'This could have been me.'

In our communities, we try to celebrate death – 'celebrate' in the sense that we do not run away from it. We look it in the face, speak of it, talk about the person who has left us, about their beauty and about our Christian hope, and also about our pain, anguish, anger or even revolt. Death is also celebrated in the way that people pray close to the dead body, support the bereaved family and live the funeral eucharist.

Some years ago now, François died of cancer in our community. He had been very much supported by his friends and helped by Father Thomas. He died a few moments after receiving Holy Communion from Father Thomas's hands. As usual, we watched over his body. Jacqueline, an assistant, met two people with handicaps who asked her whether they could see him. They came into his room and prayed together. Then they asked whether they could kiss him. 'Of course', Jacqueline said. So Jean-Louis kissed him and exclaimed, 'Shit, he's cold!' Then the two of them left the room saying to each other, 'Mum will be astonished when I tell her that I have kissed a dead person!' These two men, with their own particular handicaps, were able to encounter death without fear or drama. They were able to accept it as a natural reality. It is the way that every man and every woman is called to go. Just as life can be beautiful, so too can death.

This is not to say that some deaths are not scandalous. There are horrible massacres. There are sudden deaths which leave a terrible vacuum. But the scandal is above all for those who stay behind and wait their turn.

IV

HUMAN GROWTH

L'Arche is a place of growth, above all for people with mental handicaps. It is wonderful to see Claudia today – a young woman at peace with herself, secure, happy and able to do lots of things. When she came to our community at Tegucigalpa as a little girl, nearly twenty years ago, she seemed completely mad. Since then she has lived through a real resurrection. Many men and women at l'Arche gradually find an inner peace; they discover their identity and can then open themselves to others. L'Arche assistants grow a great deal too. They discover who they are; their lives become filled with meaning and hope. They learn to assume responsibility. They open themselves up to others, and especially to those who are different. Many find a place where they can put down their roots and where what is deepest in them can blossom and bear fruit.

Growth is at the heart of l'Arche; it is at the heart of what it means to be human. Human beings are constantly growing. They evolve, change, pass through different stages, discover their identity and open themselves to others. And this growth which begins at the moment of conception, when the first cell is formed, goes on until the moment of death, through times of joy and grief, through gestures of love and moments of action, communion and suffering.

The life that begins when a child is conceived is a powerful reality, hidden in that first cell. This life is not just a physical thing, allowing the growth of the tiny body with all its organs, but also something psychological and spiritual. The power of life hidden in the body pushes the tiny child out of the womb of his mother and into her arms, and incites him to enjoy his parents' love, to advance through life, to acquire knowledge, to become independent of his parents, to love others, to open himself to the world, to create and procreate. There are not a number of life-forces working alongside each other – one to form the body, one to create relationships and another to develop knowledge and creativity. All is united. All is one, contained in that life hidden in the first cell. It is at the root of all movement and all physical growth, but also of all relationships, all growth in knowledge, all spiritual activity.

This life is like water flowing in a river. It turns and winds. If it meets an obstacle, it flows round it. The first obstacle it meets is pain, the unbearable rock of suffering which seems like an enemy of life, a harbinger of death. Life skirts round this horrible reality; it moves on elsewhere.

The first suffering that a child experiences, which causes the first inner wound, is like a foretaste of death. All alone the child is too little, weak and vulnerable to be able to live. She needs adults to feed her and protect her against the things that are hostile in nature and society. If she does not feel loved, the child experiences the trauma of the fear of death. She is completely devastated, in a state of distress and panic in the face of this terrible reality. Life cannot bear its opposite, death. It refuses to be extinguished. It shouts, revolts, struggles to protect itself and survive. The power and even violence hidden in life enable it to overcome or bypass all that is unbearable. It does this by escaping into dreams, into plans, into relationships that are not based on true communion, relationships in which a person tries to prove himself in the eyes of others, to be admired and to dominate. So life continues to flow. If, as is the case with many people who come to l'Arche, life is not vigorous, if it has not been called forth by love, it protects itself by hiding behind depression, madness or dreams. It cannot move forward. It is as if it shuts itself off and hides. It looks from the outside as if the child is sulking. She cuts herself off from relationships. But inside, life remains hidden like a treasure, waiting to set out on its journey again if one day it is called to do so.

Growth

Contained in that first cell in every human being is an astonishing programme which will enable the child to resemble his mother, father, grandparents and ancestors. This life is passed from generation to generation, handing on skin colour, size, genetic illnesses, intelligence.

There are things in life that are predetermined – our nose is such-and-such a size – but also things that are not. Life is flexible, embracing reality, adapting itself according to its environment and the welcome that it does or does not receive. The body develops, life flows if it finds love, or else it tenses up, draws back and protects itself in the face of obstacles, fear and suffering. Defence mechanisms go up, the body develops blocks against life, or it forces itself forward with a kind of violence.

The growth which begins in the initial cell will carry on throughout life, right until the end, at least as far as love and acceptance of self and of reality are concerned. There is growth and also decline. From the age of twenty-two onwards, each of us becomes progressively weaker. From then on, every day, 100,000 cells die in the brain and are not replaced (fortunately, we have a lot of brain cells!). Every day not only the brain but also the heart, kidneys and liver shrink until there comes a time when the body gets weaker and weaker and one of the essential organs ceases to function. Life then comes to an end.

I mentioned in the previous chapter how amazed I am by the similarity between the beginning and the end of life, between small children and old people. There is however one fundamental difference. Children are not intellectually conscious; they do not exercise choice. But old age comes after a life of choices. It is the final fruit of choice. Old people enter into weakness after lots of relationships, having accumulated knowledge and experience; their heart is full of all that has been given to them, or, sometimes, empty because of the things they have not had. They move towards the final journey of death with a heart that has been expanded by love, weakened by illness, pierced by suffering, humbled by failures, so that it is ready to welcome a new form of communion.

The seed that grows

The other day at table, in my house at l'Arche, Jean-François, Christophe, Laurent and Patrick were talking about the work they had been doing in the garden and about all the little seeds, no bigger than grains of sand, that they had planted in the earth. They had covered them, watered them and fifteen days later they saw little green shoots poking out of the earth. When they looked at the seeds, they had difficulty in telling one from another: which was a dahlia, which a tomato or radish? Later, as the seedlings rose from the earth, they were able to tell them apart. Hidden in each of these tiny seeds is a life, a mystery, a reality which is not revealed until certain conditions are fulfilled. The seed needs good earth, space to grow in, water, sun, air. Different kinds of seeds grow in different ways. It takes a good gardener who knows the needs of each of the seeds and their laws of growth to help each one flower and be fruitful. And when it comes to fruit-trees and vines, the gardener or vinedresser must hurt the trees. He must cut and wound, pruning the branches so that they can bear even more fruit.

It is the same for human beings. Human growth follows precise laws. There have been children brought up by animals (one lives in a l'Arche community), but their development has not been truly human, nor are they able to communicate as human beings. For human beings to become really human, they must be brought up and loved by other human beings. Therapists versed in the science of psychology know that there are laws about human growth. If these are not respected, children will not develop in the right way, and will have difficulty in living humanly. Children have a right to receive what they need in order to become really themselves, to become human.

What is predetermined and what is not in human growth

Human beings are so different from animals! Birds fly freely, with such joy. They sing and communicate together easily. Fish swim, insects crawl, animals run. Each of them feeds and reproduces. Each has its own identity. Each is open to receiving from and giving to the entire universe. But this identity and openness is given by nature. It is instinctive.

It is not the same when it comes to human beings. As with animals, there are some physical and psycho-logical characteristics which are determined, but not all. Upbringing plays a part too, for children who have been really welcomed by their parents will find it easier to live communion and form relationships with others and with the universe. Children who have not really been welcomed will find these things much more difficult. There are other things about each human being that are not predetermined, but the result of choices and the way they have exercised free will. A person's identity is built up as a result of the many choices he or she makes in life. People choose to share their lives with certain friends, with a wife, a husband; they choose a profession, moral principles and values; they choose either to open themselves to others, or to remain closed. Obviously, psychological instincts and upbringing influence these choices.

As people grow towards establishing an identity, they are going to be influenced by the values of the culture and the circles they move in, and by their family. Through the trust they place in their parents and through all the moments of love and tenderness and celebration that they experience with them, people will receive a faith and belief in certain values. They will be in communion then with that which is most authentic and unified in their parents. Children are perceptive enough to feed themselves on all that is true and deepest in their parents. But they cannot bear what seems false or contradictory in their parents.

Where there is little in the way of communion and truth, a child can still receive a faith and values from his parents, but his attachment to this faith will be more superficial; it will often spring from a need for security and recognition. As he grows and is confronted by reality, he will either choose his faith and make it his own or he will reject it.

The meaning of life

What meaning can be found in life in the modern world? So many people today are searching, so many seem lost and no longer have any kind of ethical reference points; so many are dissatisfied with a purely materialistic life, with ephemeral pleasures or with a quest for power and success. Many of these are people of great goodwill; they want justice, communion and peace, but they do not know how to go about achieving them. Politics and politicians often seem dishonest and corrupt, religions unwelcoming and legalistic, business, industry and technology dehumanising. So many young people turn towards sects or political or religious movements which are closed up and sectarian. How can we help them to discover that our world is not bad, and that each of us can make a useful contribution towards making it a more truly human place?

Through my experiences both before and in l'Arche I have discovered the importance of two essential elements in human life that can give it meaning both for people of goodwill who have no religion, and for people who are searching for God, whatever their religion: *being*, and *being open*, having a clear identity and being open to others. We establish an identity through the place where we live, our family, culture, education and physical and psychological state. But we establish it too through our choice of profession, our gifts and abilities, our values and fundamental motivations in life, through friends, through the commitments we make and through searching for truth in ourselves and in life. Being open to others, especially to those who are different from ourselves, is to see them not as rivals and enemies but as brothers and sisters in humanity, capable of bringing light and truth into our lives, and of living in communion with us.

Openness does not imply weakness, nor a tolerance which ignores truth and justice. Being open does not mean adhering to others' ideologies. It means being truly sympathetic and welcoming to people, listening to them, and in particular to people who are weak or poor or oppressed, so as to live in communion with them.

People who do not have an identity, who have not put down roots and do not have a clear set of values, cannot be really open to others. They cannot give because they do not really know who they are, what they want and what they are capable of. Those, on the other hand, who have a strong identity, but who are closed in on themselves and on their own particular circle, behind solid walls, are convinced that they are right. They judge and condemn people who do not see things their way. Either they are in danger of suffocation, or they tend to create conflict.

Those who have an identity and who are open to people different from themselves will gradually become people of compassion, peace and reconciliation. Through humble and simple acts, through listening and kindness, they will bring peace and unity. By directing their abilities towards communion, they will help others to live their humanity more fully and to be united in love and in a common purpose. Openness also implies trying to understand those who are different, and those who use their authority to oppress people, in order to find ways of entering into dialogue with them. Openness impels us to make space for them in our hearts.

Each person has his or her secret

It is important to be flexible in our understanding of human laws, and to appreciate that there is a system of compensation built into every living thing. If, because of illness, a person's powers of reasoning are not able to develop, then his vital energy will flow in another part of his being. It is important to recognise and support this so that the person can attain the fullness of his being in his life as it is.

The first and most essential law of growth is that of love

and communion. To live fully, grow in freedom and bring life to others, a human being needs another person who recognises her as unique, and who will encourage her to grow and to become herself. Without this, she will close in on herself, become defensive, or seek to prove herself. In order to develop their full potential, human beings need a milieu of communion, trust and friendship. Sometimes the kind of communion and friendship which awaken the human heart are to found in the most unexpected surroundings: in prisons or psychiatric hospitals, among beggars or street children and women who have fallen victim to prostitution. Amongst those who are poor and broken, there can sometimes be a beautiful solidarity of love.

Every human being has his or her secret and mystery. Some lives are long, others short. Some people seem to live through stages of growth, others do not. But I believe that every person arrives at true maturity at the moment of death. It is very easy to see the purpose of some people's lives; with others it is more difficult. But I believe that every person's life is important, whatever their limitations, poverty or gifts. There is a meaning to every life, even if we cannot see it. I believe that each person, in her unique beauty and worth, lives out a sacred story. For me, a person exists from the moment of her conception. She exists even if, like Eric or Hélène, she has a profound handicap.

She exists with her particular beauty, even when, as in the case of men and women of the road, people in prison, people addicted to drugs and alcohol, this beauty is disfigured. It exists even in those who commit brutal murders, or torture others, or abuse children. Each person is important, each is capable of changing, evolving, becoming a little more open, responding to love and to communion. I would like to pass on to others this faith in human beings and in their capacity for growth. Without it, our societies are in

147

danger of becoming purely paternalistic in their attitude to those who are weaker, doing things for them rather than helping them to stand on their own feet so that they can do things for themselves and then open themselves to others. Our societies are in danger of rejecting those who disturb them too much, and sometimes of even wanting to get rid of them.

Accepting ourselves in order to grow

Each person has his secret and mystery, his particular journey, his vocation to grow. Certainly, many people never achieve full maturity, but each can make a little progress towards establishing his identity and becoming open to others. The important thing is not that we should achieve human perfection – far from it – but that we should set out on the road towards it through acts of openness and love, kindness and communion. Every person today, in whatever situation he finds himself, in his home or at work, can perform such acts.

As we have already said, there are things that are predetermined in human beings and things that are not. Identity and human growth are arrived at through choices: choices of friends and of the values we want to live by, the choice of where we put down roots, the choice to accept responsibility.

The first choice, at the root of all human growth, is the choice to accept ourselves; to accept ourselves as we are, with our gifts and abilities, but also our shortcomings, inner wounds, darkness, faults, mortality; to accept our past and family and environment, but equally our capacity for growth; to accept the universe with its laws, and our place at the heart of this universe. Growth begins when we give up dreaming about ourselves and accept our humanity as it is, limited and poor but also beautiful. Sometimes, the refusal to accept ourselves hides real gifts and abilities. The dangerous thing for human beings is to want to be other than they are, to want to be someone else, or even to want to be God. We need to be ourselves, with our gifts and abilities, our capacity for communion and co-operation. This is the way to be happy.

Not long ago a young woman told me, 'I have begun to be happy that I am a woman. Now, I really like wearing skirts.' Little by little, she was beginning to live because she was learning to accept herself. There are people who are constantly running away from themselves; they always want to have a more important, more responsible position, so they live in a state of frustration . . . until the day they discover that they can live happily in a humbler, simpler role which suits their capabilities better.

Finding a place to put down roots and to be well nourished

A plant cannot grow unless it puts down roots in the earth, good earth. It is the same for a human being. His 'earth' is his family, his human community, the community of his friends. At l'Arche, several months after the death of his father, Jean-Claude, a man with a handicap, announced when we were gathered together, 'Now that my father is dead, l'Arche is my family.' He had chosen where to put down his roots. The family communicates to a child a culture, language and values. There are rich 'earths', where people grow well, and there are poor 'earths', like the shed near Ouagadougou, in Burkina Faso, which welcomes about thirty men of the road, beggars, many of whom have mental or physical handicaps. Certainly in this rather unusual type of life there are explosions and outbursts of anger, but there is also brotherhood and sharing.

Human beings need physical nourishment, otherwise they have no energy, but they also need to nourish their hearts, their spirits and their intellects. The journey towards deepening our identity and the quality of our openness to others is long. Any one of us can sink into discouragement and apathy, closing in on ourselves, our anger and frustration, and seeking compensations which can close us up even more. We need nourishment to keep our hearts open. We also need – or many of us do – some kind of intellectual or philosophical understanding of life, of human beings. We need to develop our taste for truth.

In the Gospel, Jesus compares the Kingdom of God, the Kingdom of Love, to a seed hidden in a field. The seed, he says, is the Word of the Kingdom (Matt. 13:18); the earth is our hearts. Some seeds fall on hard ground and they cannot grow. It is like when the Word of the Kingdom falls on hearts that are hard and closed. Others fall on thin soil. They shoot up quickly, but die quickly too. These are people without roots, without depth; when they encounter difficulties, the Word of the Kingdom in them dies. Other seeds fall on rich soil, but are choked by weeds. These, Jesus says, are the seductions of riches and the worries of the world which stifle the Word of the Kingdom. Finally, some fall into rich soil and bear much fruit.

Our hearts, spirits and intellects need to be awakened and fed. When people discover their own capacity to give life and hope to others, then they want to give more. There are forces of selfishness and fear in each of us, but where there is good spiritual nourishment, the power of love rises up. At l'Arche, we recognise that if assistants are not sustained and helped to see the meaning and value of their daily lives, apathy sets in and their ability to listen and pay proper attention to others flags. But if they are well nourished, they give life.

People of communion, co-operation and competence

Communion and trust form the basis of human psychology. They are at the root of all human growth; they touch what is deepest in human beings. When we live communion, we open ourselves to others, we make ourselves vulnerable to them. We can then progress towards co-operation and collaboration. We live these first of all with brothers and sisters. There may be feelings of jealousy between children, but little by little, if a family is healthy and loving, a child discovers the joy of having brothers and sisters and of being part of a family. If he does not have these sibling relationships, the child will find it more difficult later on to open himself up to his peers. The difficulties experienced by the only child, on whom everything is centred, will remain with him. When there are brothers and sisters around, children will learn to take the knocks that come with family life, to share its daily joys and sufferings, and to be mutually supportive. They will discover that they are not alone in the world, that there are others to whom they can be bonded in friendship, and they will begin to open themselves to their peers.

This sense of co-operation will deepen at school, although it has to be said that, for the most part, schools are run along competitive lines; everyone must succeed, win prizes, come first in sports and in studies in order to feel their own worth and be admired and affirmed by their parents. Few schools are run as communities. I saw one in Calcutta where the children supported each other, the strongest helping the weaker ones. In some integrated schools in Canada, where children with handicaps learn side by side with other children, there is an education geared to community, co-operation and mutual support. Each person finds his or her place; each has a gift to exercise. Each child then discovers that differences are not a threat but something precious, and this enables them to work together. They are then no longer in a competitive system where others become rivals or potential enemies; the others are brothers or sisters with whom they can play and work. It is when we are adults in a family, a community, or in the world of work, that we discover and deepen co-operation as an important human reality. Together we can do so much more than when we are alone.

As she grows, a child discovers her particular interests and gifts: in sport, art, handicrafts, manual activities, or in different academic subjects at school. These interests will be an important part of her education and development. When she is a teenager, they will enable her to specialise and choose a career, gradually becoming more qualified and competent, at least in one area. She will be admired by her parents, those around her and her friends. Her personality will be strengthened by these abilities which need not necessarily be professional, but might be, for example, those of an excellent cook and housekeeper. We have seen at l'Arche how the characters of people with handicaps are strengthened, structured and developed through their work. They discover that they are capable of doing beautiful things.

Education is harmonious when a child, and then teenager and adult, can develop these three elements: communion, co-operation and competence. Together, they bring a person towards wholeness. Communion opens them to heart-to-heart relationships; co-operation opens them to social and community life; competence allows them to take their place in life. But some people can be seriously lacking at the level of communion. They live only to increase their knowledge and their competence. They perform efficiently. But they close in on themselves avoiding personal relationships. They enter into co-operation with people only if in doing so they can form a strong team, or company that is successful. They are obsessed by work and are unable to listen to others, to share with them and become vulnerable and open to them. In the same way, if a child is not encouraged to develop her abilities, there is a danger that she will operate only on an affective and emotional level. A time will come when she will wonder what she can really offer others.

If a person is to be able to grow towards maturity and take his place in society, he needs to invest his energy in these three areas. The overdevelopment of competence at the expense of communion and co-operation impedes true growth and leads to an unbalanced psyche. There are people who are very mature on the level of competence, but who are little children on an emotional level, crying out for love. Many of our abilities are developed during adolescence because of competition and the need to win and be admired. It is during the period of maturity that we can hope for a transition towards competence inspired by communion and co-operation. It will then become a truly human competence, directed towards the good of others.

Being well and relaxed

In order to grow towards a deeper sense of identity and to open ourselves to others, we need times of quiet and reflection, times of inner peace and relaxation. If we are preoccupied with plans and a compulsive need to succeed and be appreciated, or if we are tired, tense and stressed, it is difficult to slow down and welcome and listen to reality and to others. Our internal motor runs too fast. It is impossible to be silent and stand back from what is happening in order to consider our motives and fears. The heart's silence is blotted out by the noise of the motor. Growth demands that we are fit, well rested, and relaxed both in body and spirit. So it is important to find a healthy rhythm of life, and to know how much rest we need and the types of relaxation that give life.

I am realising more and more that there are many people who do not know how to relax. It took me a long time to learn. Obviously, people know that they must sleep, but relaxation is more than that. Sleep, moreover, can be a way of avoiding reality, an escape, a kind of depression. Real rest is the renewal of our energy so that we can struggle for peace and truth with more energy, enthusiasm and hope. So relaxation is finding new sources of energy, and being affirmed and supported in the awakening of these energies, it is rediscovering trust in our mission and what is deepest in us. It is the opposite of slumping in sadness, apathy, lack of self-confidence and doubt. Real rest involves relaxing the heart with friends and family through celebration, laughing, singing, joy, humour. It means feeling well and happy in our body, house, family and community.

Personally, I feel much better after spending the month of August in a monastery. I need the silence, the relaxation, the physical exercise and the time for prayer.

For Jews, the Sabbath is important. It is a day reserved for the essentials: for prayer, reflection and relaxing with the family beneath the gaze of God. It is not an escape from the work of the other six days of the week, but a time to refind the energy to return to that reality and there to establish peace, compassion and truth. It is important for all of us to know how to recharge our batteries.

Often at l'Arche, young assistants do not know how

to deal with physical tiredness; and physical tiredness quickly turns into psychological tiredness and stress. This psychological tiredness can then take over and become like a cancer which eats away at them internally. Physical tiredness needs to be dealt with prudently, and we need to know how to combat the onset of sadness and depression which can follow.

Stress is often the result of a lack of harmony between life's difficulties and responsibilities, and the kind of support, spiritual nourishment and formation we need to be able to cope with these difficulties. Stress can cause certain psychological disorders. In order to find relief from these, a person may become depressive or aggressive, or look for compensation in alcohol or something else. Often he becomes excessively tired or falls victim to psychosomatic illness.

In order to be relaxed and fit we also need to have found that balance we spoke about between communion, co-operation with others and the exercise of our abilities. To be relaxed, we need space – our own private space, the place of solitude where we can really be in touch with our deepest being. If we do not have this, if our space is taken away or violated, if we are under too much pressure, or overwhelmed with things to do, then we risk falling into confusion. We can no longer really welcome people to come close to us. We are unable to understand and love them. We are forced to defend and protect ourselves, because the pressure is too great. If the waters of our hearts are to run freely, and if we are to remain fully open to life, we must have that inner and outer space where we can find peace and rest. This space is different for each one of us. Some people need to live alone, and each of us needs times of solitude – these might be a day each week, a month each year, or quiet, prayerful moments during the day, which might be early in the morning or before going to sleep.

Accompaniment

In order to develop properly, some plants need the support of a stake. With this help, they produce more flowers and fruit. People also need another person to help them grow well: someone close to them who accompanies them, helps them to live their humanity more fully, to reach maturity and to give life and hope to others. This accompaniment is not just for teenagers who need a spiritual guide or mentor to act as an intermediary between their life with their family and their life in society. Whatever age we are, we need someone to walk with us. Personally, I was lucky enough to be accompanied for nearly forty-six years by Father Thomas Philippe. He never told me what to do, but he asked me questions which made me reflect about my vocation and the purpose of my life. He knew that the more the fundamental goal of our lives is clear and present to our hearts and minds, the easier it is to discern and choose the right way of reaching it.

At the moment, I do not have specific responsibilities within my community. However I do accompany a number of assistants who have been with l'Arche for varying amounts of time. I am neither a psychologist nor a priest, but I have some experience of life and of people. I have a certain knowledge of human beings and of their journey to spiritual and human maturity. My role in accompanying assistants is to listen to them so as to discover with them the cause and meaning of their difficulties both as human beings and within the community. It is important to meet them where they are and not to judge them on the basis of an ideal or of what I think they ought to become. It is important to help them to find coherence beween what they say and what they live, to live the reality of their humanity, to know and accept their gifts and their abilities but also their limitations and their inner wounds, and above all to believe in their humanity, their spiritual life and their capacity for journeying towards greater maturity through the right spiritual and intellectual nourishment, and the support and rest that they need. During these moments of communion, which are important and nourishing for both of us, I learn a lot about human beings and the stages of human growth. I am amazed at the openness and straightforwardness of most of these assistants. Sometimes what I say helps them, but on the whole it is my listening more than anything else that enables them to put their hopes, difficulties and needs into words. I also recognise that a certain number of them find it painful to think and talk about who they really are. They seem a bit afraid; the barriers around their hearts and spirits are too strong and they do not manage to articulate their difficulties and their fears. Generally, accompaniment is something very gentle. Communion is gradually built up between us, and mutual trust and a desire for the truth increase over years of meetings. I am discovering how essential accompaniment is for human growth.

The first principle in accompaniment is to help the other person to live in reality and not in dreams, theories and illusions, to accept who he or she really is, with their inner handicaps, wounds and shadow areas, so that they do not live in a constant state of frustration, guilt and stress. There is no need to be perfect. Of course, we need hope, and a vision for the future, but these are very different from illusions and dreams that have no basis in reality, that are the fruit of an imagination, cut off from reality.

I remember an assistant who came to see me almost in

tears. During the night, he had been infuriated by a person with a handicap, and a lot of violence had welled up in him. 'I could have killed him,' he told me. I was able to tell him that I too had lived through such an experience, and that it had been a turning point in my life. I saw all the potential for evil hidden deep within me. It was a moment of conversion for me. There are things in us that we cannot change all at once; it takes time. We have to negotiate with our bodies, our defence mechanisms and our particular sources of anguish.

In this way, Aristotle has been a great help to me. He was passionate about what was real and human. He led me to embrace reality. I sometimes have difficulties with Aristotelians who are obsessed with their master and his ideas, but do not follow his example in embracing reality!

But sometimes, people do not want to listen to the truth of their beings nor to look at and embrace reality. They are not ready to accept their weaknesses, limitations and inner handicaps. Then we have to wait for the right moment to help them accept their reality.

There are things that we can change in our life and surroundings, and things we cannot. It is important to distinguish between the two. I sometimes see people fighting in vain against things that they cannot change. But they fail to see the little thing, either in their life or in a particular situation, that they can change. They fail to see what is possible. Perhaps too many people today are paralysed by the world situation; they are unable to see what is possible, what they can do to make our world a better place.

In the course of my experience at l'Arche, I have discovered four principles necessary for human growth and for good accompaniment:

– *The principle of reality*: to embrace things as they really are, and not to be constantly angry with them but rather to see what is positive in them. Not to be attached to preconceived ideas and especially not to prejudices and theories. To recognise in ourselves the blind spots and the defence mechanisms that stop us from seeing reality, and lead us to deny it. To love and live the present moment in the reality that is given.

– *The principle of growth*: life is moving, evolving. There are things that we cannot do today because of our limitations, our youth, our fears. But tomorrow, or with time, new strengths will grow up in us. We are in the process of changing; others are changing too. We must know how to wait patiently. We must know how to befriend time.

– Finally, the *principle of nourishment* and the *principle of finality*. As I said earlier, the purpose of all human growth is openness to others, to God, to the world: to discover our common humanity; to work for a world where there is more communion and compassion between human beings. But each person needs to choose the right means to be well nourished in order to achieve this end. We must make good choices. Athletes and artists know that they must live a disciplined life to achieve their goals.

One of the great difficulties for some assistants is that they want and at the same time do not want to be at l'Arche. They are not always clear about their choice of life, their vocation and the purpose to which they want to devote their lives. When we are not clearly oriented to the goal, we will always find it painful to accept the means and the various kinds of loss and sacrifice it involves. If we have a clearly defined goal, then we accept more easily the discipline that comes with that life, and the rest, spiritual nourishment and the friends we need.

Times of crisis

For most of us, life is made up of crises, breakages, separations, and unexpected events which may be good but can sometimes be bad, like illnesses and accidents. Death appears to us throughout life. In Chinese, the word 'crisis' implies danger, but also opportunity. Crises may bring a threat of death, but they are also the opportunity for a new start in life, a rebirth. In Greek, the word implies the need to move forward, to make a choice in order to escape from a situation in which we have become trapped. A number of crises are brought on by exhaustion and a lack of harmony between communion, co-operation and competence. We have invested too much energy in one of the three, forgetting or avoiding the others. Nature then expresses its discomfort. A man who devotes all his energy to work, forgetting his family, will reach a crisis when his wife gets angry with him and threatens to leave if he does not change. He then has to make a choice, and find the necessary help, because his work has become an escape. He has become dependent on it as a way of calming his anguish and filling up his life. He needs to rediscover communion.

In 1976 I fell ill and had to spend two months in hospital. My body was crying out that I had mistreated it. I had not given it the rest and nourishment that it needed. This taught me a lesson. After the illness, I re-established a better equilibrium and a better rhythm of life.

There are accidents, illnesses, depression and difficult times that force a person to rediscover in himself resources that have remained hidden. There are also crises which give rise to guilt or to a growing malaise in a person's heart or conscience. They cannot bear the fact that they have had an abortion or an extra-marital sexual relationship, or that they have lied or been entangled in some form of corruption. Guilt is like a cancer which eats away at a person internally, making joy and openness impossible, standing in the way of communion and sometimes of co-operation. Then one day there is an explosion. The malaise has become too great; it turns into a cry to rediscover communion, openness, honesty. There is a strange law at work in these situations. The person is almost forced to do more and more stupid things, so that one day the truth emerges and he is freed from his secret guilt. When it comes to doing things that are evil, corrupt and dishonest, there seems to be no half-way house. We have to keep going a bit further. There are also all those people who, through fear, have failed at a particular period of their lives to grow up: the teenager who is afraid of leaving his parents and who wishes to remain a child; the grown-up who fears commitment and giving life, and wants to remain an adolescent, searching, without responsibility; the old person who refuses to acknowledge his age and grief. Perhaps because of a lack of preparation and support, perhaps because of sickness or psychological weaknesses, these people were unable to make the right choices at the right time. At a certain moment, when they have failed to make a transition from one stage of their lives into another, their anguish becomes too strong, nature cries out, and a crisis appears. There are those who have been unable to face their fears: fear of failure, of death, of being abandoned; they have spent their time running away from them. Then, one day, their fears take over. They have to look for help. The crisis prepares the way for a renewal of life.

I am struck by the number of people who are forced to

descend into the depths of despair and loneliness before they can climb back out towards life. The only language they seem capable of listening to is a violent one of sickness or death. They refuse to listen to friendly advice. Until they have hit rock bottom, they refuse help because they reckon that they do not need it. They believe that they can climb out of the abyss all by themselves. They live in a fantasy world; they deny reality. This was perhaps the kind of state I was in before I went to hospital. Often we go to the doctor too late. Is this not what happens with people who drink too much or take drugs? They deny the gravity of their situation.

A man in prison wrote me a very moving letter. He had been successful in his profession, he was married with children and he had had a good life, but it was completely focused on himself and his success. 'So,' he wrote to me, 'I did something really stupid' – he did not tell me what. Then he said, 'I was put in solitary confinement. I descended to the depths of despair. I had lost everything. I wanted to die. And then suddenly a kind of tiny star of light entered my heart. I looked at it, and took hold of it. It grew.' As a result of this experience of light and hope, this man lived a rebirth in the prison cell. Very gradually, he was transformed by a spiritual faith and the desire to open himself to others and to work for them. He had had to touch the very pits of despair before seeking help from others. Only then did he find within himself a new strength which allowed him to overcome his selfishness, his internal contradictions, his conscious and unconscious guilt, and begin to direct his life towards communion and co-operation.

So crisis is a time of danger and an opportunity for renewal, for rediscovering a new equilibrium and inner freedom. It reveals a lack of harmony and openness. It is a time to seek help from a priest, a spiritual guide, a friend, a therapist, or some other person who can help us to make good decisions, leave illusions and lies, and to see and embrace reality so as to move forward in life.

What impresses me is that despite all the falseness of life, the times of failure and irresponsibility and lack of equilibrium, human beings often find peace at the moment of death. After many bruises and much suffering, they rediscover at the end of their lives the communion and peace that they knew at the beginning. When Jesus died, he had near him, crucified like him, a man condemned to death. He spoke to Jesus with sympathy, saying, 'Remember me, when you come into your Kingdom.' And Jesus replied, 'Today you will be with me in paradise.'

A mother once told me the story of her little son who had died at the age of five. When he was three he had an illness which brought on paralysis of his legs. This spread to the rest of his body. At five he was bedridden, blind and totally paralysed. One day his mother was crying by his bedside when he said to her, 'Don't cry, Mummy, I still have a heart to love you with.' Despite being so young, this little boy died in a mature way. A sign of maturity is the ability to rejoice in what we have, rather than bemoaning what we do not have. It is a sign of immaturity to lament what we have not got rather than giving thanks for what we have. Many people die peacefully, having accepted their reality. There has been human life on this planet for millions and millions of years; there have been, and will be, millions and millions of human beings. Each one of them has their place. For many, the most important things in their lives happen in the very last moments, when, through death, they humbly accept the reality of life. Displays of brilliance, often the fruit of pride and the need to be admired, pass like the wind. Gestures of love which are life-giving and which come from the truest part of our beings are present in that final 'yes' at death, which is also a 'yes' to life – a gentle, little 'yes' of peace, acceptance, maturity and gratitude.

Pruning

In the chapter about the stages of life, we talked about times of trial and loss: the loss of dreams and of hope, the loss of work, the loss of friends. These trials are sometimes extremely painful and the heart bleeds. We seem to fall into a pit of anguish overwhelmed by a feeling of inner death; life loses all meaning. Some people – the victims of the Holocaust, for example, or of the massacres in Bosnia and Rwanda, or of child abuse – live through horrific, totally incomprehensible suffering. Some live the suffering of hatred, like the man condemned to death in prison in Montreal for having killed seven people. I saw him behind the bars, his body was rigid, his eyes fixed and cold; the atmosphere surrounding him froze and paralysed me. And yet at the same time, looking at him, I could guess what his life had been like. Probably hated from the time when he was in his mother's womb, abandoned, placed in institution after institution, he had received violence and had learned to attack others in order to live and survive. To protect himself, he had been forced to build immense walls around his heart and his emotions. How could he live in trust if nobody had trusted him? His heart was hidden behind all the ruins and barriers of his life. What terrible suffering he had undergone; what terrible suffering he had inflicted on others.

I marvel at some men and women who have suffered sometimes severe illnesses or handicaps, but who have gradually come to accept and embrace them. Several years ago, I was invited to Montreal to meet men and women with physical handicaps. I had been asked to talk to them, but when I met them I felt unable to speak until I had listened to them. I asked them to tell me their stories and how they had suffered. Each one explained the bitterness they had experienced. One said, 'I had polio when I was seventeen. To begin with my school friends supported me. Then they left school. Gradually, they stopped visiting me. Now I have no friends. I feel I've been rejected by a hard society.' One after another they talked about their pain and their anger with society. Then one woman with polio spoke up, 'How can we criticise people in society for not accepting us if we fail to accept them in their non-acceptance of us?' Suffering had brought her to a wisdom so beautiful; it was as if she had been pruned and was now bearing the fruits of welcome and self-acceptance. She radiated love. The others had not arrived at this wisdom, and were still closed up in anger, rebellion and a feeling that they were victims. Was this because nobody had accepted them with their handicaps and revealed to them their worth?

A young woman of seventeen wrote me a long letter telling me about her family life. She had suffered a lot because she felt that her parents had never really wanted her. It was as if she had been a mistake. Her parents often praised her older brother and sister, but never her. Then she went to school, but she had no friends. 'It was', she said, 'as if nobody could love me.' This young woman had been suffering from a lack of affection and was close to depression. Then, she continued, she went for a walk one day in the woods. She sat down under a tree. 'Suddenly,' she told me, 'I was overwhelmed with a feeling that I was loved by God.' It was an experience that enabled her to accept herself. If she was loved by God, then she could love herself. If she could love herself, then perhaps she could allow others to love her.

So much suffering comes from disappointment. We wait

for something which we believe will bring us happiness, and it does not arrive. We see only the negative things that have come our way – illness, a child with a handicap – and we close up in anger and rebellion. Human wisdom means coming back down to earth; not closing ourselves up in a beautiful ideal which we must attain, but welcoming reality just as it is; discovering God present in reality; not struggling against reality, but working with it; discovering the seed of life, the possibilities hidden in it. Of course we must have a vision for the future and focus on it, we must plan, and be aware of and responsible for the future, but our hope and vision must be rooted in the present. This is Buddhist wisdom, but also Christian – to discover God in the present moment, to be a friend of time and of reality.

Life is not memories and longing for the past, nor is it dreams and fantasies about the future. It is here and now, flowing with and from reality, in communion with the earth, the universe, other people and ourselves, and it flows from reality.

When I was in Bangladesh, I learned a beautiful lesson. After I had given a conference for a group of parents and friends of people with handicaps, a man got up. 'My name is Dominique,' he said. 'I have a son, Vincent, who has a severe handicap. He was a beautiful child when he was born, but at six months he had a terribly high fever which brought on convulsions. It affected his brain and his nervous system. Now, at sixteen, he has a severe mental handicap. He cannot walk, or talk, or eat by himself. He is completely dependent. He cannot communicate, except through touch. My wife and I suffered a lot. We prayed to God to heal our Vincent. And God answered our prayer, but not in the way that we expected. He has not healed Vincent, but he has changed our hearts. He has filled my wife and myself with joy at having a son like him.' Reality is not always changed. But by a gift of God, our barriers and preconceived ideas fall, doors are opened within us. A new strength surges up permitting us not only to accept reality but to live it peacefully and even to love it.

Becoming ourselves

Whatever our path in life, whatever crises and difficulties we suffer, what really matters is that we should become ourselves, not paralysed by fear of others and what they think, or by our psychological needs for tenderness and power.

Not long ago, a nineteen-year-old assistant from a l'Arche community came to see me. I asked him how he was getting on. He told me he was doing all right, but that it was hard. I asked him to tell me something good that was happening. He said, 'I am becoming myself.' Through all the stages of growth, is not the real aim in life to become ourselves, to allow the barriers to come down so that the deepest 'I' can emerge? Not to become what others want us to be, not to cry out to get their attention at any price. Not to refuse life, or to try to be someone else, but to grow from the seed of life within each of us, rooted in our earth and history. Is this not our journey home?

This emergence of the real 'I' – this refusal to compromise with a world which crushes weak people and personal freedom and conscience, this refusal to compromise with evil and forces of corruption and oppression – seems to be particularly hard in public life. Pontius Pilate knew that Jesus was innocent, but he did not dare set him free for fear of causing a revolution, arousing the Emperor's anger and losing the position, honours and privileges which meant everything to him. When magistrates sell their conscience and soul to political powers and tyrants in order to win their favour, not only does their deepest 'I' not emerge, it is dissolved by fear. When we commit an injustice through fear of losing our position or good name, when we lie because we are afraid of conflict or rejection, when we accept bribes, the 'I' is plunged deeper and deeper into the dark areas of our being.

Sometimes young people are put under great pressure to take drugs, or to follow the crowd. If they refuse, they are laughed at, mocked as cowards. Bullying can make life at school unbearable. You need to be strong to say 'No', but it is then that the deep 'I' emerges. In the same way, it is not easy to make a stand for justice and truth in our workplace, or in certain tyrannical regimes. But the 'I' emerges when we speak the truth, when we are brave enough to risk stepping out of line, and finding ourselves on our own. When we denounce injustice simply to gain honour and recognition, the 'I' does not really emerge. Healing takes place every time we choose truth and justice and follow our conscience.

The emergence of the 'I' does not give us a freedom of power, the freedom to judge and condemn others and think ourselves better than them. Nor does it give the freedom of independence, the capacity to do whatever we want; nor the freedom of a saviour. It gives the freedom of vulnerability, the capacity to suffer with others, to listen to them so as to understand their pain. It is the freedom to take our own place and not anyone else's in society and the universe, so as to live communion and compassion, and communicate trust and freedom to others. It is the freedom to submit to a truth and justice that is greater than ourselves and our group, and which allows us to be in communion with universal and eternal values. It is the freedom to be ourselves.

The emergence of the 'I' takes place in humility, gradually, through all sorts of set-backs and even mistakes. It is a slow and beautiful growth through all the stages of life. As we travel towards it, we are called to be patient, to find the rhythm proper to our growth, trusting in time and allowing all the things that happen to us – illness, crises, the things we read, encounters, separations and bereavements – to do their work gently within us. Where there is a real desire to live in truth, everything will work together for the good of the person and for his or her growth towards human and spiritual maturity.

So the growth of a human being towards a deeper identity and greater openness corresponds to the emergence of the 'I'. It is not something big and strong. It may not even be possible to see it happening. It does not bring honours or financial reward. It is something that happens inside ourselves, something to do with love and fidelity in love, something to do with justice, trust, communion with others and welcoming others. This growth in communion takes place particularly in people who are humble and socially unimportant. Those who are important and powerful will also become unimportant at the end of their lives, but during their time of 'importance' and power they are taken up with their need to exert this power. Human growth involves acquiring certain things, but it is realised above all in service, in solidarity and in giving. It is a school of giving. We learn how to give, to give our hearts. And the final gift, in which everything is accomplished, is the gift of our heart as we welcome the God of gifts, who in turn welcomes us into his arms.

Living in today's culture

We have moved from a world governed by a morality based on the family and on religion, to a world governed by individual success, material aquisitions, power and personal fulfilment; from a sense of duty to others, to our country and to God, to a quest for our own well-being. Psychology and economics have taken the place of morality as our top priorities. From a world in which customs and morals were rigid and unchanging, we have moved into an age of complete liberty in which anything goes and rules and morals can be abandoned, into a society in which communication is supposedly paramount, but which is, in fact, taken up with the search for stimulation rather than true relationship. Despite the fact that it has some good programmes, television is responsible for a real confusion about values, about what brings real fulfilment and wholeness to human beings and what does not. It makes everything seem possible. An important medical professor admitted in the newspapers that, while he was practising as a doctor, he used to kill premature babies with handicaps. I wrote to him protesting in the name of life. 'You are certain about these things,' he replied. 'I am still searching. You claim to know the truth; I would not dare claim that.' Almost the same remark was made to me by a French writer who had agreed to put his twenty-one-year-old daughter who had Down's syndrome on the pill so that she could have sexual experiences. What both these people were really saying to me was, 'Your certitudes show you are a fascist. You want to impose rules on others.' But is morality not first and foremost the defence of the rights of people, and above all of those who are weakest, of their right to life, to a home, to an education, to care and love? Is it not the way to wholeness and true happiness for each person – a way to bring them to inner freedom?

If we deny morality, then that is the end of all true education, of respect for every person no matter who they are. It opens the door to all kinds of injustice. The world becomes a jungle in which we each defend ourselves as best we can.

It is important to emphasise the importance of morality, but we can also hide behind laws. We can crush and kill people in the name of law – or we can let people destroy themselves and others through the absence of law. There are the laws inscribed in nature, which every doctor and psychologist knows well. There are also the laws of a society. Law is, or should be, there to help people – every person – to journey to a fullness of life and to be truly free: free from prejudice and fear, free from a paralysing selfishness, free to love and be compassionate, free to struggle for justice.

Our world is in turmoil – people are tense, worried and insecure. They tend to fall into a state of human, cultural, intellectual and spiritual poverty. Many people are overwhelmed by images and information. Out of necessity, they are living on a superficial level. Most have neither the time nor the desire to discover a road, possibly a new road, to peace and true human fulfilment. They are completely caught up in the demands of daily living, the need to find work and to earn more money. They tend to want everything, and to want it immediately. They look for powerful and exciting experiences to make them feel alive. In a situation like this, it is difficult to refind real guidelines to life. The kind of supports that used to exist are no longer there, and anyway life is so different from what it was before and it is impossible to go backwards.

Humanity continues on a journey that is both beautiful and disastrous. But, as I believe that the universe and humanity have been well made, that they contain within them elements of balance and healing, there is undoubtedly another way which is unfolding and which will help each one of us, all of us together, to find a new equilibrium and inner peace. This new way, which is unfolding, will certainly lead human beings to the discovery of a communion that is deeper than fleeting experiences; a communion that

171

involves permanence, covenant, fidelity; a communion that is creativity, liberty, light and life; a communion that is celebration. And this new way will lead to the discovery of a God not 'up there' in the heavens, whom we can only reach through self-denial and obedience to laws, but of a God of love hidden like a tiny child at the heart of creation, at the heart of human suffering, at the heart of daily life.

V

A HUMAN ENVIRONMENT

It took me time to discover where I should put down roots, where I would be able to grow in love, protect and strengthen my identity, live fully my gifts, give life and open myself to others – in short, to discover the role that environment plays in human growth.

I was fortunate in my family. My childhood memories are happy ones. Obviously, we five children had fights, but there was also a real friendship between us. Our parents gave us great security, and I cannot remember any conflict between them.

In 1942, in the middle of the war, I left my family and Canada to enrol in the British navy. In those days it was possible to go to naval college, the school where future officers were trained, at the age of thirteen. I left naval college at the beginning of 1946 to serve in warships. Like the French and Canadian navies, the British navy is a powerful institution in which there is a great sense of belonging. We were proud to be in the navy and we loved the whole way of life in warships. There was a bond of real friendship between the officers. The uniform, the traditions and the naval trappings created a strong *esprit de corps*. Personal life, meanwhile, was kept to a minimum. The way of life strengthened in all of us a spirit of courage, hard work, loyalty, honesty and co-operation.

After I left the navy to follow Jesus in 1950, I discovered

the spiritual life and began to study philosophy and theology. I was living in a community near Paris, founded by
Father Thomas Philippe, but I was more of a loner than
a member of the community. I was happy in this life of
prayer and intellectual pursuit, even though it was fairly
austere. I hid myself behind a kind of inner strength that
the navy had developed in me. I tended to shy away from
relationships in order to devote myself completely to my
spiritual life.

It was only with the beginning of l'Arche, in 1964,
that I discovered community and community life. At
the beginning, as the founder and person responsible
for the organisation, I lived a bit on the outside of the
community. But as the years went by, I began to discover
the deep significance of community, and how essential it is
for human growth. L'Arche is not a religious community
as such, nor is it a professional organisation based on
competence and efficiency. We are more like a big family,
united by a common spirit, mutual trust and love.

It was clear to me that Raphael and Philippe's most
fundamental need was not to live independently and be
completely autonomous – their handicaps made that
impossible. What they needed was to become part of
a new family, to be able to join in with the life of a
community where they could develop their human and
spiritual potential as fully as possible in a spirit of freedom
and openness. They needed people who would walk with
them for the rest of their lives, not for financial gain but
out of freely given love. Through living with them, I found
that their need corresponded to a deep human need hidden
within me.

In the early years of l'Arche, I visited institutions for
people with mental handicaps in many countries. I needed to
know what was happening in other places. In Scandinavian

countries, I met men and women with mental handicaps living in their rooms or individual apartments with their own television and bottles of beer! This was presented to me as the height of successful normalisation and integration! They were certainly better off than the people in the big institutions and psychiatric hospitals that I had visited in France, but somehow life seemed no longer to flow in them. Shut off in their lonely rooms, they seemed sad and introverted, psychologically cut off from life.

We all need friends. They are our security; with them there is the to and fro of mutual support. We can exchange ideas with them; we can take the risk of really living.

I am told that in Paris 40 per cent of people live alone. All these people are forced to protect themselves. They have to defend themselves against all society's hostile influences. In 1980 an American sociologist coined the expression 'cocooning' to describe this need for protection. Now, this same sociologist is witnessing a new escalation of fear. It is no longer enough just to protect ourselves; we have to resist aggression. So city-dwellers are starting to hide away in their homes. At work, people are forced to develop their aggression, which is often expressed through competition. They have to demonstrate that they are abler and more competent than others in order to be promoted and get pay rises. Exhausted by the stress of work and by commuting to and from work, they have little energy left to put into relationships and into building up the human community. They try to distract themselves by watching television, which is one of the ultimate forms of loneliness. This serves to accentuate the loneliness of their lives, and the difficulties they have in communicating and opening up to others.

Gradually, through living in l'Arche, I discovered how essential the human community and the family are as intermediaries between individuals and society. These are the places where each of us can become who we really are. Barriers protecting our vulnerability can be allowed to fall so that we are able to open up to others, and in particular to people who are different from ourselves. Communities and families provide the 'soil' in which we can put down our roots; without good 'soil', we cannot live and grow as human beings.

People in society

Today's society is complex. In order to be really integrated in it, a person needs to be trained and competent. This enables him to have a job and a salary. These, in turn, enable him to have a personal and family life, to develop leisure activities and friendships. Life in society is governed by the laws of competition. At the top of the social hierarchy are the 'winners'; those who are strong and capable. At the bottom are the 'losers', the weak who need help. Everyone seeks to climb up the ladder of human promotion so as to have more privileges and money; those who cannot climb up tend to sink into despondency.

Natural communities, such as the family, have been weakened in our rich, modern society. The media has contributed to this weakening by constantly offering new and powerful experiences. Competition, the drive for individual success and wealth, the philosophy of personal freedom and the loss of moral and religious values have also played their part.

In his book *Les Exclus* (or *The Outsiders*), René Lenoir talks about young American Indian children in Canada. He describes a group of twenty children to whom someone had offered a prize for the first one who could answer the question, 'What is the capital of France?' They got together

178

to exchange ideas, and then shouted out in unison, 'Paris!' Why did they do that? Because they knew that alone there was only a one-in-twenty chance of winning. They also knew that the person who won the prize would somehow no longer be part of the community; he would be above them all. In our rich societies, many have won the prize at the expense of losing the sense of community and solidarity. In poorer countries, they have not won the prize, but they have often managed to retain the sense of solidarity.

Community life begins sometimes as friendship. We spend our free time with friends. We can relax with them and allow our masks to fall. It is all right to be ourselves and we can do what we like; we are not constrained by rules. But friendship also implies commitment. Of course, it can remain superficial, free of mutual responsibility. When the other person no longer seems interesting or important, we can go elsewhere and allow the friendship to lapse. But a true friend feels responsible for his friends, during bad times as well as good, in success and failure, humiliation and sorrow. So there is commitment. It is the beginning of living community. Friendship without commitment is not true friendship.

Every human being needs friends. Raphael and Philippe, like all of us, needed friends who would stay with them, despite their handicaps, and would make a commitment to them for the future. Families or communities are the places where we make mutual commitments to share our lives together and support one another. They are the places where we meet people on the level of the heart, become vulnerable to them and share the experiences and joys of life. There are schools and institutions which develop our minds, but communities and families are schools of the heart, of love and of faithfulness to others. These schools teach us to be more open to others, especially to those who are different from ourselves, as well as helping us to learn about forgiveness and universal love.

I am particularly conscious these days of the suffering of men and women whose marriages have broken up, and whose hearts are broken as a result. There is a danger of their losing confidence in themselves and in their ability to live in relationships. Sometimes they throw themselves too quickly into other relationships, because they cannot bear to live alone. These people need friends who will walk with them, and sometimes a good counsellor, to help them to look back over what has happened to them, and to recover confidence in themselves. Then, gradually, their wounds heal, they discover that it is possible to live positive and loving relationships which are a source of life for themselves and for others.

The dangers of friends, families and communities that are too closed and inward-looking

Friends can shut others out so the relationship becomes unhealthily introverted. They flatter and support one another. Among themselves, they can cultivate a sense of superiority, a kind of disdain for others. But, through friendship, we can also encourage each other to be more open to others, to risk loving and struggling for justice.

In the same way, families can be open and hospitable to others, and especially to those who are different. They can prepare their children to become good and responsible members of society. Or families can become very closed and shut off from other people, places of mutual protection, jealously guarding their possessions and inheritance. Is that not why in certain Asian and Latin American countries, 10 per cent of the population owns 75 per cent of the land? Obviously, in this kind of situation, wealthy families can help the poor in a paternalistic way, taking care of them when they are ill or in dire need. However, they do nothing to share their land or wealth, or to change an unjust situation. We can understand the reaction which can come from the anger of those who are oppressed and who see the family as a 'bourgeois' reality that supports the rich. They then seek to weaken or even to break up the family.

In the same way, there are communities that are closed in on themselves, convinced that they are right, élitist. The most extreme examples of this are sects. It is important to distinguish true communities from sects, particularly for us at l'Arche which is sometimes accused of being a sect. A sect is rigorously closed in on itself. Its members, often insecure and fragile people, exchange their freedom and individual consciences for a collective conscience, formed by a father or mother figure, or an all-powerful guru who is often seen as an envoy of God. They are fed with fears and prejudices as a means of preventing them having contact with others who do not think like them. For them, the world is divided into the good and the bad, the saved and the damned. Between these two groups is a huge wall, and no contact is allowed with people on the other side of the wall except to proselytize. There is no room for self-criticism. These fragile people caught up in sects are seeking the security of order and want to impose it on others. There is a resemblance between sects and certain kinds of fascism and dictatorial regimes. Both are determined, at all costs, to stop people from exercising personal liberty; they see this as a bad thing that would lead to anarchy and disorder.

I have to admit that in the early days of l'Arche, I paid little attention to our neighbours in the village. I looked after our own affairs; I had my project welcoming Raphael and Philippe. We were rather cut off and did not try to have much outside contact. Perhaps at the beginning, a community has to be a bit closed in on itself. Its new life and still fragile identity have to be protected. But I gradually learned how important it was to be open to neighbours, to talk to them, and not to be closed in on ourselves.

Unlike a sect, a true community exists for people to help each other grow towards maturity and inner liberty, so that they can become responsible for themselves and others. If at the beginning, authority in a community is quite heavily imposed on its members, it is called to evolve into an authority which helps each one to grow and become him- or herself. A true community is open so it can give life to others outside: visitors, neighbours, friends and people who are different. It is called to take part in the life of the area or region in which it finds itself. But in order to give life to others, the community itself must be alive.

For a multitude of reasons, communities to which people used to belong, like families, villages and parishes, are nowadays tending to break up, and even disappear. More and more people are alone. Is it not essential, then, to encourage the creation and growth of places of belonging? If these intermediaries between people and society, these schools of the heart, do not exist, people will find it more and more difficult to achieve maturity.

The challenge of l'Arche is to be an institution that is competent, even professional, in the way it helps people with handicaps to find equilibrium and develop their potential, and at the same time to be a community in which all the members – people with handicaps and assistants – are bonded in love and live in communion. Is this possible? Normally, institutions are organised along hierarchical lines and those employees with greater responsibility have higher salaries. There are labour laws which fix responsibilities, privileges and salaries. Trades unions protect people at work. All this is good and efficient, but it does not foster community life, nor the formation of permanent bonds between people.

Because it proclaims a vision of community, l'Arche has had to find another way of regulating salaries. Everybody gets the same pay, except married couples who need to rent or buy a house. Similarly, people are given positions of responsibility for limited periods, normally four years, after which they are frequently called back to work more closely with people with handicaps. There is a logic in this which everyone recognises. In the l'Arche vision, it is more truly human to work close to people who are weak and to live in communion with them than to work in positions with greater responsibility and higher salaries. Each person is called to serve the community according to his or her gifts and abilities. Each freely chooses the community with all the joys and sacrifices that this implies, rather than choosing to live in a hierarchical institution with its advantages and inconveniences.

Is it possible that l'Arche can be a model? Is it possible to imagine hospitals, schools and even businesses run more along the lines of communities? Is it always necessary to have hierarchies of salary which separate managers from the workforce, desk workers from manual workers?

A human community: people meeting each other

One of the most fundamental needs of human beings is that of communication and communion. But so often, as we have seen, trust gives way to fear. 'Hell is other people,' Sartre said. With another person, there is a risk that we will be consumed, controlled, possessed, that we will become unduly submissive. So we must either engage in a subtle struggle to consume, control and possess the other, or else we remain hidden, scared, sad and sure that we are not lovable; we turn ourselves into victims and allow ourselves one day to be consumed. Either we journey towards openness, communion and trust, or we withdraw into ourselves in fear of others. A truly human society must help people to move towards openness. A society cannot be truly human if everybody is afraid of everybody else.

When I talk about community, I mean all associations of human beings who not only have some goal to achieve – like people in business, the army or a sports team – but who also help people to meet one another on a personal level, where there is dialogue, sharing, openness and a true concern for others. Even though their initial intention was perhaps to form a powerful group in a competitive society, these people have also learned to trust one another and to help each one to become more fully him- or herself.

Society should encourage associations like this, just as love and loyalty are encouraged in a family. The citizens of Eastern Europe, and especially of the former USSR, have suffered greatly under regimes that sought to stamp out associations like this and to destroy trust between people. They followed a policy of divide and rule. I have seen in these countries how long it can take for people to trust one another. They need time to become open to each other after all these years of repression.

But it is not only in the countries of Eastern Europe that there is a lack of trust between people. How quickly, even in l'Arche, we can divide members of the community into those in whom we have total trust and those we do not completely trust. Similarly, we can very easily encourage competence and efficiency at the expense of encouraging people to come together to share on a personal level.

There are many kinds of human community, working at different levels. Sometimes commitment to the community is something official and expressed, and sometimes not. Two things are essential: the meeting of hearts and individual support for each person, and a common goal for which people come together. People who play cards or darts, teachers in a school, a medical team, people working together in business, those who come together to struggle against torture, or to work for peace with non-violent methods, or for more responsible attitudes towards our environment, and lots of other kinds of groups besides, can gradually become little communities that encourage people to meet on a personal level, and to become responsible to one another. In the same way, spiritually motivated groups, such as prayer groups, charities to help homeless people, and Bible study groups, can either gradually become communities or they can move further and further away from being true communities if all their energies are directed to the goal that brought them together and not to mutual caring.

In these different kinds of community, people's loneliness is eased; there is sharing and caring for one another. People no longer have to prove things about themselves. They have the right to be themselves; they can let go of their defence mechanisms. They can open up to one another in communion. There are bonds of love between them.

These groups become even truer communities when they are no longer inward-looking and élitist, when they open themselves to others outside, when they are aware of their mission to give life to others, and above all to people who are lonely and distressed, and to work with other communities and groups for the good of the whole of society.

Obviously, communities like l'Arche, where we live together under the same roof, particularly merit the name 'community'. But they are exceptions in our societies. For people who need a great deal of personal space, such a community life can be impossible. But they can be part of a community without living in it all the time.

The mission of Faith and Light is to help very loosely formed support communities to start up and to grow and deepen. About thirty people, people with handicaps, their parents and their friends, come together once or twice a month, and also sometimes for holidays. These communities are places of communion, sharing, celebration and prayer. I can vouch for the radical change they have brought about in their members. They have been places of much inner healing and human growth.

The family is the most common and most natural of all communities: a man and woman committed to one another and to their children. Here too we find the two elements essential to community, the meeting of hearts and common values. If the marriage is founded simply on a desire for intimacy as an escape from loneliness, and not on a certain ideal of shared life and real communion, then it will be in danger of breaking down.

It is in the nature of a community, whatever its type, that it should become more and more a single body. It is no longer a hierarchy governed by competition where the strong are on top and the weak on the bottom, nor a superficial friendship free of responsibility. Each person, weak or strong, has his or her place in a community. Each has his or her particular gifts and no one is 'better' than anyone else. The analogy of the body that Paul uses to describe the community is very good. In the human body, he says, there are many parts. Each is different, each important, and 'the weakest parts, the ones we keep hidden, are necessary to the body and should be honoured' (1 Cor. 12). All the parts, each with its own identity, are bonded together. They belong to one another. They have a responsibility and commitment to one another.

The joy and pain of shared life

Leaving behind loneliness and no longer being afraid of our weaknesses and poverty brings great joy. Love, friendship and openness to one another are some of the greatest human riches. This joy is greatest of all at the start of a family, at the time of a marriage, when a person realises that she has been chosen by another, not for her abilities but in her deepest being, and chosen for life! Here the joy of intimacy, ecstasy and love, the deep need for security, the fulfilling of our capacity to give life, and our need to have a status in society are all brought together. The Wedding Feast is an expression of human bliss.

And yet at the same time, especially today, the family is so fragile! The values of rich societies which encourage personal experience and independence, the fact that often both husband and wife work in exhausting and stressful jobs, their human and psychological development over time which can lead them in different directions, the painful discovery of differences and the lack of support available for couples, all contribute to the pressure on a marriage and sometimes make life together almost impossible. After a time, the strain from these difficulties can cause the breakdown of a family.

It is the same with a community. From the outside, it can seem such a beautiful place of sharing, co-operation, mutual support and so on. But as soon as we are inside it, we quickly begin to see others' faults! At the beginning, we idealise others. Then, as we get close to them, we begin to see only what is negative. We have to pass through these stages in order finally to meet people as they really are, neither angels nor demons, but human beings, beautiful but wounded, a mixture of light and darkness. These are the people with whom we have made a commitment to live and grow together.

I think that in human relations, there is always a danger of picking and choosing. We enjoy being with certain people, they are interesting, charming, funny, intelligent, they give us life. But little by little, the novelty wears off. They begin to reveal other aspects of their characters, sides of themselves that are possessive, aggressive or depressive, that wound and can provoke anguish. When difficulties arise, there is a danger of wanting to finish the friendship and simply drop that friend, unless, of course, there is some kind of mutual commitment and responsiblity which makes us work at the problems in the relationship. It is the same in a community.

We choose our friends, but we do not choose our brothers and sisters. In the same way, our companions in a community are not of our choosing. This is where all the difficulties of community life begin, because among the members of a community, some people attract us – they are sympathetic, they share the same ideas, sensitivity and vision. But we find that others rub us up the wrong way – they are disagreeable, they have different ways of doing things, different attitudes, characters, senses of humour, views about community life. They wound and provoke anguish; their presence is stifling, or their attitudes annoy us.

In Luke's gospel (Luke 10:38–42) he talks of two sisters, Martha and Mary. One is organised, strong, controlling. The other, who is younger, is loving and hyper-sensitive; it is in her nature to build up relationships. The two women can either wound and inspire fear in one other or, by recognising each other's gifts, they can complement each other. In community life, there is a transition to be made between seeing others as rivals, threats, people to be jealous and afraid of because they have gifts that we do not have, and seeing them as members of the same body, different from ourselves, but important and necessary to the life of the body. Differences then are no longer a threat, but a treasure.

Community life can become a real school for growth and love; it reveals differences – differences which irritate or are painful; it reveals the wounds and shadows inside us, the plank in our own eye, our capacity for judging and rejecting others, the difficulty we have in listening to and accepting others. These difficulties can lead people to run away from community, to cut themselves off from those whom they find unsettling, to become introverted and refuse to communicate, to accuse and condemn others; or it can lead them to work on themselves, to struggle against selfishness and their need to be at the centre of everything, so as to welcome, understand and serve others better. When this happens, community life becomes a school of love and a source of healing.

A true community is moulded by a unity that comes from the inside, through mutual trust and a sense of inner freedom, and not from the outside through fear. The unity springs from the fact that each one is respected and finds his or her place. There is no more rivalry or jealousy. This community, united by a spiritual force, radiates peace and is open to others. It is neither élitist nor jealous of its power. It desires simply to fulfil its mission, with other communities, to be a force for peace in a divided world.

Making the transition

Joining a community is never easy. It implies real loss and grief. People who get married have to prepare themselves for the loss of personal freedom. Often they do not prepare themselves for this very well. The joy of the wedding, of putting an end to loneliness and of at last being chosen by another as a companion for life, is such that they forget to look at what they are losing, their private space and a part of their personal freedom. Moving into family life, or into community life, is a tremendous change. There are real demands in community life: decisions cannot be taken alone; there are gatherings and meetings that must be attended; there are ways of reflecting together. There are the demands of having to be ready to listen to people, and even greater demands when somebody in the community becomes weak, or falls ill or into depression. The honeymoon can turn into a storm!

There are some people who get married, or join a community, simply in order to escape their own problems. Sometimes, couples join a larger community in order to escape their problems as a couple. When they discover that the community cannot solve their problems, there is a danger of them accusing the community and becoming a problem both in and for it. Neither community nor marriage are the answer to all problems. They are places of healing and growth. But good 'accompaniment', a spiritual guide, and sometimes even psychological help, are necessary in order to avoid a catastrophe and to ensure that the transition from the utopian ideal to reality, the reality of others, of the community and of ourselves, takes place harmoniously.

And with all its joy and pain, the community is not the be-all-and-end-all of life. Everybody dies alone. Each of us has to leave the community one day. And sometimes human communities ossify and shut themselves off from the outside world. They can become places where the group gets rich and where people protect one another and hide their mediocrity. Then they are no longer places of growth but of death; everyone demands that the community be attentive to themselves, but nobody really wants to be attentive to others! There is not just one moment when the transition from 'the community for me' to 'me for the community' is made; it has to be remade every day. The community is not the solution to all human problems and sufferings; it remains a challenge. Every one of us, every day, is called to grow and to make new sacrifices, to progress towards greater self-giving. And sometimes, in order to live in the truth, it is necessary to know when to leave the community, or even to accept rejection by it. The theologian Bonhoeffer (who was executed by the Nazis) said that Jesus, the great founder of community life, died alone, away from his community, surrounded simply by a few friends.

Embracing difference

I have said that families are schools of the heart, schools of love, where we learn, sometimes through anguish and fear, to embrace difference. These days there is a tendency to erase difference and say that everybody is the same. This is both true and untrue. People with handicaps, and especially people with severe handicaps, are very unlike other people, even if fundamentally they are the same in that they need to love and to be loved, and to fulfil their potential. But their ways of understanding, of communicating and of loving are very different. In the same way, men and women are different in so far as their emotional needs are concerned, their ways of approaching reality and of exercising authority.

It is above all at l'Arche that I have discovered how mutually complementary men and women are. When I was the leader of the community, I always had a woman sharing responsibility with me. In other l'Arche communities, where a woman is the leader, we have seen that things work better if she has a man sharing responsiblity with her. They complement one another. Men need women and women need men. Of course, this is a generalisation. There are situations where the lack of a person of the opposite sex does not lead to any problems. I can only talk about my own experience of the fact that men and women are complementary. It is good for men and women to work together, with their different emotional make-up and different ways of expressing anger.

The differences between men and women are first and foremost in their bodies and sexuality. The woman welcomes – her sexuality is more internal – whereas the man's sexuality is external. These biological differences have their repercussions on the psychological level. When a man exercises authority, he thinks more about structure, about devising a plan that will enable him to achieve a project. A woman is more concerned with people. The man is more reasonable, the woman more intuitive, finer, more delicate, more attentive to detail. These differences, which I have experienced a thousand times, are obviously not absolutes. There are the Marthas and the Marys. Men can be intuitive and women reasonable. What is important is to find a harmony between the masculine and feminine, where one does not dominate the other.

Often, a man tries to use his strength to dominate a woman. He refuses to acknowledge the quality of her intelligence and he does not listen to her. He seeks power. But if he takes time to be open and listen to the woman, the man discovers how beautifully their natures complement each other, and the joy of their coming together to form the body of the family or the community. He then undergoes a real transformation. He no longer focuses simply on himself and his own success. By himself, he has not got access to full wisdom and truth. And it is the same for the woman. The man and woman need each other. This transformation, which often takes place in the context of the family, has an effect on everything a man or woman does and everyone they meet. Inherent in it is a realisation that we all share a common humanity; we do not need to win in order to exist. We are not fully independent. Other people are not rivals but partners. The purpose of life, then, is not to climb up the ladder, trampling on those we leave behind, but to help each person to discover his or her unique place in the body of the community, to recognise each person's gifts but also their particular difficulties.

Because it is a place where people meet each other at a deep level, the community is also a place where hearts are healed. Through working closely together within the community, we discover all the difficulties and wounds we have when it comes to relationships. Wisdom lies in the discovery of who we really are, with all our limitations and hidden weaknesses. Having discovered them, we can then look for help and support. From idealism, we can fall into pessimism, but then, later, we can rise up, more anchored in reality.

True unity cannot be achieved in a family or community which denies difference, and behaves as if everyone should be the same and think in the same way. Unity is achieved when each member of the body is different and contributes a different gift, but all are united around the same goal, by mutual love. For this to happen, each of us must be in the process of being purified of our need to excel and to prove that we are best. We must all seek to open ourselves to others and welcome their gifts; we must be ready to become vulnerable to others. Unity is something we all have to work at constantly.

I was very struck by the unity between a couple at l'Arche,

the tenderness and attention they showed each other after
twenty years of marriage. I told them how important their
unity was for l'Arche. 'It wasn't always like this,' the
husband said with a smile, 'We had to work hard to
achieve unity.'

The role of weak people in building up unity
in the community

L'Arche communities are rooted in the relationship of love
and trust between people with handicaps and those who
have chosen to live with them. The open, smiling faces
of men like Marc or Albert touch me deeply. Their trust
draws me to them and brings forth new energy in my heart.
I do not want to, and I could not, let them down. They are
like an anchor for me. They help me to be true to what I
really am. They call me to stay with them and not to allow
myself to be seduced by power, popularity or ambition.
The covenant we live together is a gift from God. I believe
that most assistants who come to l'Arche have this same
experience. People who are weak help us to discover what
is deepest in us. They help us on our journey home.

I have also discovered at l'Arche the joy of trust between
assistants. It is wonderful to have lived all these years with
so many brothers and sisters. But we all know that the
foundations of our community and of the union between
us are the people with handicaps. Without them, we would
not be together. With them, we discover we can give life.
Their happy faces and relaxed bodies reveal to us who we
are. They are not possessive or clinging. They enable us to
trust, and we enable them to trust. They know that we have
things to do or a mission to be accomplished. Because they
are sure of the bonds that unite us, they allow us to leave,
knowing that we shall always return.

Families come into being in a different way. A man and a woman are attracted to one another, and their mutual attraction leads them to want to start a family, to have children. After the honeymoon period, full of joy and ecstasy, communion and deep intimacy, perhaps before the emergence of any real difficulties in the relationship, there comes the conception and birth of a child. There is the extraordinary joy of being able to say, 'My child', of being a source of life, of seeing the child's smile, her trust, her tiny body, of holding her in one's arms and playing with her, feeling maternal or paternal love welling up, watching her grow up and discover the world. It is then no longer just love and mutual trust, but also the new paternal or maternal energies that keep the parents together. The little child helps to foster unity.

But all this is not simple. The child cries in the middle of the night. She brings out her parents' aggression, and, if they have different ideas about how she should be brought up, she may create conflict between them. Similarly, things are not always simple with people with handicaps at l'Arche. People with handicaps also arouse aggression and can sometimes cause division. All these difficulties can lead to crises, which present us with both risk and opportunity: the risk of separation, or the opportunity of discovering a new and deeper unity. Children and people who are weak call us to grow and to become more responsible. They also call us to unity and so help us to overcome superficial differences in order to discover something deeper.

The community: a place where sexuality becomes integrated

It is not easy for human beings to live their sexuality. In marriage, more than anywhere else, the integration

195

of sexuality is achieved with the greatest harmony. In marriage, the body, spirit and heart, passion, tenderness and kindness, the ecstasy of the present moment, and security and faithfulness for the future, intimacy, communion and the desire to give life all come together. Before, and even sometimes after this wonderful time, there is discord between the heart which thirsts for communion and for loyalty to one person, and sexual fantasies and desires. Many good husbands have spoken to me about the difficulties they have in this area, and their attraction to younger women. The integration of genital sexuality is never an easy thing. It is a slow process which requires effort and clear choices, a communion in love, tenderness and concern for the other, and the help that comes from God.

When I talked about adolescence, I pointed out how internally divided human beings are. They both thirst for and fear communion, permanent communion. They have sexual desires that are to a greater or lesser extent divorced from true relationship. In thirty years of community life, I have noticed that a community is one of the places in which human beings can recover inner unity, provided that the members of the community are deeply united and loving, that they celebrate their unity, that they have a clear code of ethics and a spiritual life directed towards communion with God and with others. Monasteries and convents provide the same kind of experience. They are places where each member of the community, through gentle love and attention, learns to integrate his or her sexuality.

Running away from relationships by throwing oneself into intellectual, manual, artistic and sporting activities, or by exercising power and seeking honour and praise, does not help people to integrate their sexuality; rather it enables them to control it by rejecting it and directing their energies elsewhere. Sometimes this is necessary.

Community life is essentially a life of relationship, communion, tenderness, listening and friendship. It is a school of the heart which, if it is motivated by a search for communion with God, goes a long way to answering the deep need for communion in the human heart. It can bring about a radical transformation in people. The life of relationships, of love of people, becomes a source of unity for people both individually and collectively. This journey of growth takes time, and obviously there will be falls along the way, but it is a journey towards wholeness and fullness of life. Where there is not a true community life, built on personal sharing and celebration, a person may lack inner unity. Because that person has not found relationships of real communion within the community, there is a danger that he or she will look elsewhere for communion as a form of compensation, but these may be but caricatures of communion.

In l'Arche, we live together – men and women, assistants and people with handicaps in the same houses. Obviously, it is not all easy. We are not naive. There are difficulties, especially for the younger assistants who have not yet worked through these questions, and who think that true relationship requires physical intimacy, even when there is no permanent mutual commitment. Sometimes, these young people come from broken families and this has caused a certain brokenness within them. It takes them time to discover the road to wholeness, the strength of communion of the heart and of a spirit stronger than sexual desire, and how community life, a spiritual life and a clear ethical code can help them on this journey.

I am amazed to see how life in a mixed community, full of life-giving activities and of relationships full of love and celebration, is a source of equilibrium for many people with handicaps, how it helps them to integrate their sexuality. Slowly, men and women who have lived through all sorts of sexual experiences in psychiatric hospitals, and who have been deeply disturbed by them, recover their equilibrium.

All this confirms in me the conviction that genital sexual activity that is cut off from a permanent communion of the heart and spirit is a source of division in human beings. A life of permanent communion of the heart and spirit is a source of unity and equilibrium and makes possible the integration of sexual desire and fantasy. It is not surprising that in a society where the natural places of belonging are becoming fragmented, people too become fragmented, and there is a growth of all kinds of sexual deviance. In a society that does not encourage real communion between hearts, the desire for imaginary communion built on fantasy is unavoidable.

The body of the community, a place of culture and celebration

Where there is communion, there is celebration and joy. To see this, just look at a mother with her child, or a young engaged couple, young married people or the joy in an elderly husband and wife after years of loyalty and love. They are happy to be together. There are parties, holidays, birthdays and special outings which relax the body and open the heart. Human beings need celebrations. L'Arche and Faith and Light communities specialise in them! Meal times in l'Arche houses often take the form of celebration and laughter. We rarely discuss serious matters; we are not terribly intellectual! Of course, there are times when we have to be serious, to discuss and try to understand the meaning of things. But more of the time is spent telling stories, laughing, playing jokes, doing things that draw people together and help them to relax. Celebration and communication through joy are particularly important for men and women who have grown up with the sense that they are a disappointment to their parents. Celebration reveals to them the joy of being together. Through celebration we can say to them, 'We rejoice that you exist, just as you are.'

Celebration creates unity in the community, and also flows from it. When a business is particularly successful, or a team wins at some sport, or someone is promoted, there are prizes and applause and honours. The winners are regarded as the best and the strongest. But celebration springs not from the fact that someone has won or proved him- or herself to be the strongest, but from the fact that the members of a community love each other, are happy to be together, each taking his or her place. Celebration flows from the union of hearts and from mutual trust.

A community that does not celebrate is in danger of becoming just a group of people that gets things done. It becomes an institution. It is not really a community. Where there is mutual trust and love, people want to open themselves to one another, to celebrate and be together. This celebration is expressed in smiling and laughter, in simple sharing, in mutual concern and sensitivity, and in the way that people relax when they come together. But it finds its fullest expression in shared meals, good meals with good wine. Words like 'companion' and 'to accompany' have their roots in the two Latin words *cum pane* – to share bread, or food. Aristotle says that for two people to be friends, they must eat a sack of salt together; they must share many meals.

Most people's first experience of communion is feeding from their mother's breast. While the baby feeds, the mother rejoices in her body and heart. Eating together is a sign of communion and friendship. Of all celebrations, meals are the most essential.

Every day there are times of relaxation and celebration, but in the course of the year there are also special celebrations: birthdays, marriages, births, baptisms, Christmas, Easter. Then there are big anniversaries: golden weddings or anniversaries marking particular moments in the history of a person, a family or community.

At l'Arche, we seize almost any opportunity to celebrate. We have birthday parties which show the person whose party it is what a gift he or she is to the community, and express our joy in his or her existence. We have celebrations to mark the foundation of the community, we reread the sacred history of the community in which there have been moments of Providential intervention, and remind ourselves of the community's *raison d'être*.

Celebrations are also an expression of the ultimate purpose of humanity. We are made for communion and celebration, for the joy and blossoming of every person. The Bible talks of the end of time as a wedding feast between humankind and God where there is ecstasy, joy and celebration in God.

Celebration is, first and foremost, a song of gratitude, a thanksgiving. We are not alone. We are all part of the same body and there is no longer any rivalry or competition. We are together in unity and love. The greatest of humanity's riches does not consist in money or possessions but in loving and united hearts, the strong supporting the weak while the weak call forth the true humanity of the strong as they help them discover their hearts and their compassion. So celebration is like a prayer that flows from unity between people; it is a sign and a source of unity with God and of the inner unity in each person. The Eucharist, which is at the heart of all Christian celebration, means 'thanksgiving'.

Celebration is something profoundly human, using all that is beautiful: songs, music played on different instruments, dance, decoration, special clothes, flowers, scent, food, wine. The whole of creation comes together in a song of joy and unity.

Of course, no human community is perfectly united; there are conflicts, shadows and fear in every heart. There are always members of a community who suffer and feel marginalised. Celebration signifies one part of reality. It signifies hope, and a desire to continue to work for unity and peace.

The danger nowadays is that people no longer know how to celebrate and eat together. In some families, everybody eats at different times. They are all busy with their own projects and people they have to meet and they bolt their food down. In order to create unity, to live as a body, we need to know how to take time over meals, to eat well with good wine or beer. We need to know how to tell stories, our own stories, and to laugh and sing together. Today, people go out drinking, they go to the cinema together, but they have forgotten how to celebrate and to communicate. Though lively celebrations are still to be found in some villages in Africa and elsewhere, village fiestas, with dancing, singing and traditional clothes are on the whole a thing of the past. We should not weep about what is gone, nor try to revive it, but each family or community should rediscover how to celebrate communion of hearts, human solidarity and mutual trust and belonging.

How can families and human communities be helped to benefit from Sundays and holidays so as to become communities of celebration? Television is a great seducer; with so many different channels, and so many different desires and needs in each person, it can destroy communication between people. Because it tends to make people passive, it can destroy personal creativity. We must learn to find games to play together, to discover talents and actions that draw us together. If we work forty hours a week, then there is time to prepare celebrations and parties. But we have to want to do it, and not succumb to apathy. Celebration is like a song of hope. To celebrate, we need hope – hope in the beauty and goodness of human beings and in their capacity to open themselves to love. At the same time, celebration rekindles hope.

Every person needs a community

So community life is not something extraordinary; it is not just for a small élite. It is something which many people live, though often they are unaware of it and do not therefore manage to deepen their sense of community and benefit from it as fully as they might. Business meetings can become friendlier and more personal. Secretaries can be seen as people with hearts, instead of as machines. When we begin to love and respect people, we communicate joy and bonds are formed. When we share at a deeper level, when we make a commitment to other people, we become responsible, we journey towards human maturity. We become more human and we discover community. We also discover celebration.

Every community, and every person, is called to evolve. There are stages in the lives of families and of communities. There is conception and birth, then childhood and adolescence, then maturity. After thirty years, l'Arche has moved into a period of maturity. Every community is called to discover and deepen its identity, what it is, what it is called to bring to others, its vocation and particular charisma. And it is called to open itself to others, to work with them, to be a source of life, peace and unity for others in society.

VI

CHOOSING PEACE

In order to change and to become more open to others, we must first recognise that we need to change. If we do not recognise this, if we consider ourselves perfect, then we are not going to set out on the journey towards inner healing. We only go to the doctor if we are ill and know it, or if we need a check-up. In the same way, what gives us a desire for inner healing is an awareness of our prejudices, the difficulties we have with our sexuality and relationships, the divisons and blockages within us, the problems we have in communicating, and our fear of others and the anger they provoke in us. This desire for change becomes stronger when we want to grow in love and compassion, to live communion and co-operation, to be true to ourselves and to choose peace.

To be truly human we must exercise our gifts and abilities as fully and competently as we can. But if we do this just to build up our own self-image, reputation and power, and not to serve others, then there is disorder. There is disorder when we are prejudiced, when we make errors of judgment about others, when we are incapable of forgiving, or of listening to and welcoming strangers. We die inwardly when we shut ourselves off behind the walls that protect us. Life ceases to flow. We no longer give life to those around us.

Sometimes, the awareness that we need to change grows out of an awareness of the gravity of the conflicts in the world, in society, at work and in our families. Are human beings condemned to continual conflict, to hatred and war? Is peace possible? How can we renounce the spirit of competition and criticism that leads to the use of force and looks on weakness and difference with contempt?

If we are to work for unity and peace in the world, we must begin at home. I have really learnt this at l'Arche. How can we help to make peace in distant countries if we are waging wars at home, with our family or neighbours, at work, at school or in our own particular human community? Working for peace in distant places can be a way of running away from ourselves and refusing to look at what is broken within us and around us. Working for peace means welcoming the people close to us, those who annoy us or disagree with us, and seem to put us down, people who provoke anguish in us. It means neither judging nor condemning these people because, like us, they are human beings who want life and peace but also have their brokenness. They are not first and foremost enemies, but brothers and sisters in humanity, wounded like ourselves.

When we deny our particular inner weaknesses, we remain in an illusion. Human beings are all so complicated. We are body and spirit and we are heart and mind. We are searching for communion, but also for independence and success. Physically, we are close to the earth; but through our intelligence, we are close to what is universal. We each have our own personal history, and our family roots. As a child, we will have experienced love and rejection. In later life, we will have known both success and failure. We will have given life, and also refused to give life. We are all a mixture of light and darkness, trust and fear, love and hatred. Division sets in when we refuse to accept and address the reality of our past, our inner wounds, our prejudices and fears. Very quickly then we either begin to deny our lack of love, or become incapable of recognising it. We deny reality. We escape into ideas, theories, dreams and plans to which we devote all our energy. We try to justify ourselves and prove our worth. We seek recognition. We are afraid of any kind of criticism, of anything which reveals our failings. It is as if the recognition of all our darkness and weaknesses would bring forth unbearable feelings of anguish and death.

We are all wounded on different levels. For some of us, there are deep wounds caused by terrible experiences in childhood: sexual abuse, fear of having been a cause of death and division for our parents, fears because we seem to have been crushed and frightened by our parents. These fears, angers, rages and even suicidal desires had to be hidden away behind solid barriers, deep in the unconscious. To survive, we had to forget them. They form an unbearable world of guilt. But a time will come when this world of pain and anguish will begin to provoke reactions that are unbearable both for ourselves and those around us. To be freed from them, we will need a good therapist.

Then there are the wounds that are found in each of us. There is the world of the subconscious formed from our thirst for communion, from our first experiences of love, and also from the fear of communion arising from experiences of rejection as children. We have to forget the latter in order to go on living. These wounds are not so deep as the first ones I talked about, and the barriers around them are less solid. They manifest themselves in our difficulties in relating, in our fears, angers and irrational actions, in a compulsive need to be loved, to prove ourselves, to be right, to win at all costs, to be admired.

There are also wounds resulting from the various stages of life: from broken relationships, losses which we have not been able to cope with and which have brought on a kind of depression or emotional paralysis, or wounds caused by an imbalance in the search for competence, communion and co-operation. If these wounds are to be healed, we need to find somebody who will accompany us and help us to look at them. Lastly, there are the wounds springing from moral guilt, which I talked about in the chapter on adult life.

In the world of darkness hidden behind the walls surrounding these wounds, there is anguish, guilt and anger. Anguish is both the cause and the product of guilt and anger, but it is also an intrinsic part of existence. Anguish is a feeling of inner death. It arises because we are not God but are mortal, because we do not have within us all the resources for fullness of life. We are limited, very limited, and we are in constant need of others. Anguish takes the form of an inner malaise, an energy with nothing to focus itself on, turning round and round on itself. It sweeps through the body, bringing agitation and confusion, and a feeling of inner emptiness which we seek to fill at all costs – with noise, food, alcohol, work, television, art, company, and imaginary worlds. It sometimes brings excruciating chest pains and a feeling of being unable to breathe.

It is not always possible to control the feeling of inner emptiness and anguish, but if we have someone to accompany us, they can help us to live in a way that is not destructive but constructive. We can learn to fill the void with things which help us to progress towards life, freedom and peace.

We touch here upon the source of our inner divisions and contradictions. We want, and we do not want. There is within us a subconscious force influencing our activities. We are not completely free. We discover that even in what appear to be the best, most beautiful or most spiritual things we do, there is an element of self-seeking and flight from pain. We discover that all the difficulties we have in relationships, and all our prejudices, spring from this world of shadows inside us.

The road to inner unity or wholeness begins as soon as we start to recognise this broken and chaotic world in the depths of our being. We no longer deny our past mistakes, our share of responsibility for things, and our infidelities. We begin to open the door of our hearts in a desire for truth and reconciliation. Most of the time, we need the kind of accompaniment we have talked about – from a person who can listen to us and help us to accept ourselves as we are and to live in truth. In doing this, we come closer to being able to forgive others and also ourselves.

Inner healing and peace come gradually as we penetrate these shadow areas without being completely overwhelmed by them, as we learn to live with anguish without falling into depression or self-hatred, anger or guilt. On this road, it is important to continue to do things that give life to others, to work for justice knowing that our motives will always be mixed. They are mixed because we are human. Regaining inner unity means acknowledging these subconscious forces, discovering that life is not to be found in external success and projects, in being admired by others or possessing things or people who fill our inner emptiness. It means recognising that escaping into distractions, or denying reality through a need to forget, cannot be life-giving. Wholeness can only come as we desire to live in the truth, to put aside falsehood, appearances, illusions and seductions, and as we face up to reality both inside and outside of ourselves with trust and humility. It is then the 'I' emerges, our real person, our personal conscience that has been more or less hidden behind psychological instincts and fears that urge us to succeed, possess, distract ourselves or to slip into sadness. It is then that we learn to accept emptiness, to live with it in a constructive way; it is then that we find inner peace and joy.

So we begin to recognise that the depressive or guilty feelings that arise from the shadow world are separate from the 'I', our true person. We need no longer say, 'I am worthless, I am bad', but rather, 'These feelings of death, sadness and lack of trust in myself are resurfacing again.' When we distance ourselves from these feelings of death, we can begin to live again. We have hope.

But where do we find the strength to break the cycle that pushes us compulsively towards success, aggression or depression? This strength comes only in the present moment when we give priority to our inner motivation for love, justice and truth over the false values of success, possessions and honour. (The latter lead to another kind of death, the death of that which is truest and most light-filled within us, our capacities for love and communion.) This strength is born and deepens through new or renewed relationships in our family or community, in discovering that we are truly accepted and loved as we are with all that is beautiful and broken within us. The barriers around our heart then begin to fall.

It is then that we return to earth and begin the journey home into ourselves, refinding the source of our lives. It is a kind of landing, an incarnation. It is the transition from the skies of dreams and illusion, theory and ideals, to reality, to acknowledging our personal history, our life, our mortal body, the world in which we live, to acknowledging others just as they are with all that is beautiful and broken in them. Whether we like it or not, we human beings are all on board the same boat of life; we are all the same, with our beauty, our thirst for peace and communion, and also with our wounds and fears. We are all part of the same humanity. So it is better that we try together to create an environment that fosters life and not death. As we rediscover our body and the body of humanity, we can open ourselves to the world of suffering around us, to those with broken bodies. We can dare to talk about ourselves and to listen to others. We no longer need to pretend to be anything other than we are. We discover that we can love others as we are and give life, not in a brilliant, successful, heroic and admirable way, but in a small, humble and very human way.

This transition or conversion often begins when we meet a person who recognises our profound beauty, who appreciates the secret of our being, hidden behind our faults, fears, false values, and who sees all the potential for life contained in this secret. In a film on the life of Jesus, Mary of Magdala, who is traditionally seen as a woman who was a victim of prostitution, says of Jesus, 'He looked at me as no other man has ever looked at me.' Women who are prostitutes are experts when it comes to the expression in men's eyes, expressions of desire, or of fear – fear of their own sexual desires. And Mary of Magdala was seen by Jesus in her secret being, in that part of her which longed for true love, which was pure and innocent, thirsting to be seen as a person and not as an object.

In my own case, this meeting took place with Father Thomas when he welcomed me after all my years in the navy. I felt that he knew me and all that was good or bad inside me, my secret self – that he loved and accepted me just as I was. This was a liberation for me. I did not have to wear a mask, or pretend to be intelligent or good. It is marvellous to be seen and recognised as a person with a destiny and a mission.

It is marvellous to feel that somebody has confidence in us, that we are not judged or condemned, but loved, that we do not have to prove ourselves, that we can allow the masks and walls to fall. There are moments of communion that bring back memories of these moments of happiness, ecstasy and communion that we experienced as tiny children. This new experience of love soothes the wounds of the past, renews trust in ourselves and releases new energies of hope. Instinctively, we can all recognise the look of love that penetrates through to what is deepest in us, just as we recognise the seductive, false looks and attitudes of people seeking to use or control us. With a human and spiritual guide who does not judge or crush us, but rather trusts and encourages us to move forward in life, we can rediscover communion. The guide is there not to suppress our freedom, but to strengthen it.

It is healing to be able to say everything to this person whom we trust, to be fully welcomed by him or her with all that is wounded and broken in us, with all that has, in the past, been a source of guilt. Talking is liberating. Daring to speak because we know we will be listened to and understood is the most realistic way of making the barriers around our heart fall. These walls are founded on a fear of being rejected, crushed, judged or condemned; they force us to go on the defensive. Talking in an atmosphere of trust liberates the child hidden inside us. At last, we are free to be ourselves with our past; we no longer need to remain hidden.

For some people, it is a godparent, an aunt, a friend, a priest, a psychologist, a teacher or a spiritual guide who is able to provide this kind of listening, to help us to see our true value hidden behind what we think of as the disaster of our life. It is this communion which enables us to see others as our brothers and sisters in humanity, and no longer judge them. It gives us the courage to communicate with people who have hurt us, and to help them to be reborn in hope, to recognise their beauty and accept their woundedness.

This communion incites us even more to bring to life that which is deepest in us, the secret of our being.

Awareness of God in ourselves

Jesus is terribly critical of those who pretend to obey the law, and who do virtuous acts just for appearance's sake; they want to enhance their own self-image, to be seen as holy and to have spiritual power. 'Woe unto you, scribes and pharisees, hypocrites. You are like whited sepulchres, beautiful on the outside but inside full of dry bones and rottenness. You give the appearance of being just but inside you are full of hypocrisy and iniquity' (Matt. 23:27-8).

The whole of chapter 23 of Matthew's gospel needs to be read to see how strong Jesus is in his attitude to those who use religion in order to gain spiritual power, and who do not live what is at the heart of religion: love and compassion, justice and faith. It is sheer hypocrisy to do charity work, or work in humanitarian organisations, or to associate with people with handicaps, without really caring for people, but rather out of a need to be praised and admired, and to have power.

I am well aware of this trap for myself. When I give talks about the poor and the weak, I am often praised. People admire me because of l'Arche. Of course acts of justice and truth should be recognised; but how quickly we become attached to honour and praise! How to remain true in this area? In Chapter 5 of Matthew's gospel, Jesus condemns not only those who kill, but also those who actively desire to kill and who vent feelings of hatred and anger. He condemns not only those who commit adultery but those who actively desire other men's wives.

We can only journey towards wholeness and unity within ourselves, with others and especially with those who are different from us, through ceasing to care about appearances or what others think of us. For that we need to find our centre, the source of our life hidden behind inner barriers and our defence mechanisms.

One of the organisations I most admire, because I have seen the effect it has on people, is Alcoholics Anonymous (AA). Its mission, and the mission of all the organisations related to it, is to liberate men and women from addiction to alcohol. In order to achieve this liberation, people who are addicted need first of all to want it. Then they need to become part of a group with whom they share, in all honesty, their struggles and everything that is broken in them. They also need to submit and abandon themselves to a higher power or energy that comes from God. Finally, they need to discover their own capacity for giving life to others, in supporting them in their struggle against alcohol.

AA recognised very quickly that behind the desire for alcohol – which for some is in the blood and very much a physical desire – there is an enormous need to escape from their own anguish, inner dis-ease and feelings of guilt. Men and women addicted to alcohol seek to forget through drinking. So if they are to be liberated from their addiction, they will have to be able to confront this anguish, to look it in the face and talk about it. This requires support from others in the group, perhaps a special therapy, and faith in a higher power which can give them the strength to say 'No' to alcohol. They need to discover that at the centre of their being, behind all the depression, God is present. Hidden behind the ruins of their past, and their inability to face up to situations, life is there waiting to blossom. They must look after this inner life, which is like a treasure hidden in the field of their being. There lives the little child, the innocent one, searching for love, tenderness, purity and communion; there is the secret person. But this life is so fragile! For so long it has been shut up behind the prison bars of their being. It is like a newborn child that needs to be surrounded with a lot of love and tenderness. It is easily frightened, and needs help to avoid slipping back behind the barriers of its shadows.

For some, abandoning themselves to a higher power means praying. But prayer is not, first and foremost, *saying* prayers. It is opening the most intimate part of ourselves to God. It is discovering that in the deepest part of our body and our being there is a source, and that source is God. God is the power that unites the universe and gives everything meaning. God transcends time. But God is not just a power, an energy or a light. God is a person with whom we can communicate and live in communion, a person who can satisfy our thirst to love and be loved, a person with whom we can enter into an intimate relationship. God hides quietly inside each of us. God does not want to force himself upon us or to curtail our freedom. He waits for us to turn towards him opening our hearts to hear him say, 'You are beautiful, but you do not know it, or you have forgotten how beautiful you are.'

I have a feeling that this God, hidden in everything and above all in the heart of every person, is pained by how he has been misrepresented in some of the images and statues that have been made of him through the ages. Poor religious education has played a part in this misrepresentation. People have invented a dictator-like God who lays down laws and is quick to punish, a hard God who makes us feel guilty for not following his law. We have made a God who approves of religious rites and external appearances, but who seems to ignore the human heart. The true God is the God of life, hidden in the deepest part of the human heart. God is a person: a father, a mother, full of tenderness; a beloved who welcomes us and gives us rest. She neither judges nor condemns. She is not, first and foremost, a God of law but a God of communion. She is the God of the poor and the weak revealed through and in Jesus. And Jesus is there to love, encourage, affirm and forgive every human being, and to make each one of us free. He is there like a spring of water ready to gush forth. Jesus came to show us the face of this hidden God: 'Come to me all you who labour and are overburdened, and I will give you rest' (Matt. 11:28). 'If anyone of you is thirsty, let him come to me and drink' (John 7:37–8).

In one of our communities, there is a man called Pierre who has a mental handicap. One day somebody asked him, 'Do you like praying?' He answered, 'Yes'. He was asked what he did when he prayed. He answered, 'I listen'. 'And what does God say to you?' 'He says, "You are my beloved son".'

The discovery of this God is like a spring within us, from which we can drink and refresh ourselves, and in which we can bathe. Finding this God within frees us from the need to look for external affirmation or to prove ourselves. It frees us from internal prisons of sadness and lack of confidence so as to rest in this source of life and in a life-giving communion. It is the discovery that beyond and beneath everything and every law, communion is possible, a secret communion with this hidden God who frees and brings to life our true person, the real 'I' – a communion which is joyful and life-giving. Once we have discovered this new power inside ourselves, we need to be disciplined to keep in touch with it. There are times when prayer is a call, it is joy and we feel drawn towards it. It is a warm light, it is communion and rest. But there are other times when this hidden God hides herself once more behind our anguish, fear and need to prove ourselves. Then we have to be disciplined and to place ourselves again and again before and in the heart of this hidden God, and to cry out for help.

To discover God in our own heart is to grow. As we have seen, human beings are characterised by growth. And growth is slow. Behind our strong inner walls are hidden our primal fears and anguish, but also the source of life. The walls are made up of our selfish and self-seeking attitudes, our need to protect ourselves from everything that devalues us, and our need to have power, possessions and immediate pleasures. It will take time for these walls to fall, as the hidden strength of life flows through us from our inner source, and permeates the whole of our lives. Once the transformation has begun, it requires perseverance and time. It will involve pain and suffering. In order for the vine to bear fruit, much fruit, the branches must be cut and wounded. They must bleed.

This communion with God and with the secret source of our being is not confined to the so-called spiritual, to the delight of inner peace. It will lead us towards the poor and the weak, towards real communion with them.

The search for the humble, the small, the different

Inner healing takes place and manifests itself when a person begins to change his habits of looking constantly for power, success and superiority, and of rejecting certain people or groups of people. As I have said, human beings in all cultures establish hierarchies. At the top, there are those who are successful, honoured, privileged, powerful; at the bottom, the good-for-nothings, the incompetent, the poor, the useless, the people with handicaps. This hierarchy can also be found between the sexes, or between races, religions, nationalities, and between people with differing levels of physical or mental health, intelligence, capacities or education. In general, all those things that bring people power – money, ability and strength, for example – are seen as better than powerlessness or weakness; intellectual work is seen as nobler than manual work, just as the mind is seen as nobler than the body. Psychological barriers confirm this hierarchy. They are created to hide weakness and guilt and to prove the excellence of strength.

So these walls or barriers must be weakened in order to free people from prejudice and this sense of hierarchy, to free the source of life in people and enable them to open themselves to others' gifts. For this to happen, we must go in the opposite direction, the direction of meeting and communion with those whom we previously looked down upon, rejected, or ignored.

This meeting with people who are limited and different and poor, with people of another class or race, often begins with gestures of generosity and then grows into listening, dialogue and communion. At the beginning, it can seem difficult, even impossible. We are so different from these other people! I experienced these difficulties myself at the beginning of l'Arche. Meeting people who are different can disturb our value systems and convictions. Welcoming them requires openness. It means starting from the assumption that he or she is a unique person, a real human being, a brother or sister with whom we share a common humanity.

But when we approach a person who is different or in special need or who is particularly vulnerable, and try to penetrate our own walls of fear and prejudice to meet them, possibly with the help of a third person, our hearts can be touched. Then compassion is awakened. For the first time, we see the other person as someone like ourselves. We do not judge her, but begin to understand her suffering and what she is living. She is a human being; she has a heart and sensitivity that have been wounded. This communion, or meeting, is a beautiful and mysterious reality. It is as if for a moment the defence mechanisms fall. Both sides find themselves in a state of vulnerability and openness and they do not know quite where it will lead them. They discover in the meeting a presence of God. They both see that they have nothing to give except their heart, their friendship, their presence. Each is poor before the other. And this happens with few words, through the eyes and touch. It is then that we discover that within the other person, with her vulnerability and differences, there is a light that shines. In listening to her, we are enriched; we have entered into a new relationship with the other person and with God. It is a moment of communion which is a source of healing for both.

But we should not idealise the poor. I know this from my experience at l'Arche. Many have been horribly wounded through conflict, oppression and rejection. They have suffered too much violence and pain. People have lied to them too often. There are not always these beautiful moments of communion. They are often angry or depressed. Sometimes, the first moments of a meeting can be gentle but then impossible expectations and elements of distress come to the fore. It is impossible to fulfil their expectations, because their longings are too great. Anger wells up, and there are explosions.

Being healed by the weak

When I see a powerful, efficient, competent man coming home from work and getting down on all fours to play with his children, laugh with them, become a child with them, I say to myself that this father is really human. He does not regard his children from on high, from some pedestal of

219

authority and knowledge. He allows himself to be touched by their littleness.

At l'Arche and in the Faith and Light communities, we do not seek first to be there *for* people with mental handicaps, but *with* them. We try to create bonds, to laugh, celebrate life and be happy together. Of course good teaching is important, of course there are things that we can teach people with handicaps, and of course we must care for them well. But what are needed above all are bonds of communion, and friendships in which people are vulnerable before one another. Then there can be a meeting of hearts which becomes a celebration. The poor person is no longer poor. She discovers that she is capable of giving; she can give joy and life, and she can make others happy. We touch here the mystery of communion.

Jesus asks his friends and disciples not to invite members of their families, rich neighbours and friends to eat with them, but those who are poor, crippled, weak and blind (Luke 14:13). 'If you do this,' he says, 'you will be happy; you will be blessed by God.' In the language of the Bible, to eat at the same table as the poor, the 'useless', is to become their friend, to enter into communion with them. This is what we are trying to do at l'Arche and in Faith and Light.

A leader of one of our communities told me about his mother who suffers from Alzheimer's disease. She had become completely dependent and weak. She could no longer eat or dress herself alone, or even brush her teeth. But the person this man wanted to talk to me about was not his mother but his father. He had been a strong, efficient, hard-working man, more concerned with success than with people. But when his wife fell ill, he did not want to put her in hospital. He kept her at home, and it was he who cared for her. It was he who helped her to eat and who brushed her teeth. 'And now,' the man told me, 'my father is completely transformed. He has become a man of tenderness and kindness.' This does not mean that the father was no longer capable of being efficient. He had begun to develop other aspects of his being: his tenderness for a defenceless person, his ability to listen, understand and be in communion with people.

Tenderness does not mean sentimentality and a show of emotion. It is unthreatening gentleness and kindness which shows another person that we consider them important and precious. Tenderness is revealed through gesture and tone of voice. It is not weakness, but a reassuring strength transmitted through the eyes and hands. It is revealed in the attitude of the body, completely attentive to the other's body. It does not impose itself and is not aggressive; it is gentle and humble. It does not issue orders. Tenderness is full of respect. It is not seductive. It is a listening and a touch which awaken energies in the heart and body of the other. It communicates life and freedom. It gives a desire for life. Tenderness is a mother who gives her little girl a bath, revealing to her that she is beautiful. It is a nurse who touches and tends a wound so as to cause her patient as little pain as possible.

Tenderness is not in opposition to competence and efficiency. On the contrary. When a young man is helped to eat, or is given a bath, it is important to be competent and efficient. He cannot be allowed to fall, or be hurt, or be left dirty! Tenderness and communion should encompass competence.

One day, I was looking at a man with a handicap. In his hand, he held a tiny wounded bird. He had made his hand into a little nest, neither so open that the bird would fall out, nor so closed that it would be crushed. The nest was a reassuring place in which the bird could grow so as to fly one day to freedom. A mother's arms are a nest for a child, not to possess or imprison him, but to give him security so that one day he can fly away. Tenderness is like this.

We are used to being told that weak people need strong people. This is obvious. But inner unity and healing come about when strong people become aware of their need of the weak. The weak awaken and reveal the heart; they awaken energies of tenderness and compassion, kindness and communion. They awaken the source of life. It was the little woman with Alzheimer's who awoke the deep spring of life in her husband. She called forth his true self and his deep 'I' from behind the barriers protecting his heart and his need for power. In embracing his weak wife with tenderness, the husband, the strong one, had begun to welcome his own weakness, the child – the wounded child – inside him. Through this he discovered that he had the right to have failings and weaknesses, that he did not always need to be strong, to win, succeed and dominate. He could be vulnerable. He did not have to wear a mask, or to pretend to be other than he was. He could be himself. This transformation involves a succession of inner deaths, suffering, possibly moments of rebellion. It is not easy. It requires time and constant effort to remain faithful to communion. But this leads to the discovery of our true humanity, and so to a deep inner liberation. In discovering the beauty and light hidden in those who are weak, the strong begin to discover the beauty and light in their own weakness. And more than this; they discover that weakness is a place that favours love and communion, it is the place where God dwells. They discover God hidden in littleness, and this is an even greater liberation.

This is the discovery at the heart of l'Arche and Faith and Light communities. It is this that gives them a precise and clear spirituality and makes them at once both very new and very fragile. This discovery cannot be structured or enforced. It is not a kind of law; it is a free gift. People who are weak communicate and call forth a presence. In my community, we welcomed Antonio, a man of twenty-six. His body was small and broken. He could neither walk, nor talk, nor eat alone. Physically, he was weak and constantly needed to be given oxygen. He did not live for long but, while he was, Antonio was a ray of sunshine. When we approached him and called him by name, his eyes shone with trust and his face burst into a smile. He was really beautiful. His littleness, his trust and his beauty touched people's hearts; people wanted to be with him. Poor and weak people can disturb us, but they can also awaken our hearts. Obviously, Antonio was demanding; he was so poor. He needed constant and competent support day and night. He needed to be washed and fed and to have people close to him. But at the same time, he awoke the hearts of assistants; he transformed them and helped them to discover a new dimension of humanity. He introduced them to a world, not of competition and action, but of contemplation, presence and tenderness. Antonio did not demand money, knowledge, power or position; he demanded communication and tenderness. Perhaps he revealed a face of God, a God who does not govern all our problems by force and extraordinary power, but a God who longs for our hearts, who calls us to communion.

Antonio was a striking example of someone who revealed and called forth communion. With other people, this revelation is less obvious. There are people with handicaps who need interesting, paid work. They want a certain independence and autonomy. We have to help them to achieve these, even if their abilities are limited. But at the heart of these people too there is a power of trust in others and a call to communion that people who are fully developed on an intellectual and manual level do not always seem to want. The strong want power. They tend to close in on themselves. It is this trust in others that should be nurtured and embraced, because it opens us to communion. In people with mental handicaps there is a greater thirst and desire for communion than in others whose handicaps are less visible. This is the mystery of their being; they have fewer barriers and are less proud. Like Antonio, though in a different way, they both disturb and awaken.

Other people with handicaps may be more anguished. They are trapped in the obsessive fears of their childhoods. Their thirst for communion is deeply hidden behind solid walls; they have a real fear of relationships which does not make things easy either for them or for those around them. Their fears, their blockages and, sometimes, their violence, frighten people. They awaken anguish more than communion. But if we seek to understand the way that they function and communicate, and if we are prepared to accept initial rejection, we gradually discover, under all their fears, their hearts thirsting for communion.

Violent people who have been very wounded by being abandoned share this thirst for communion. Sometimes they have such strong feelings of anger and rebellion, and such a capacity for manipulation, that it is not easy to approach them. Their thirst for communion is hidden behind thick walls. Meeting them in truth requires an inner strength and a group of people who can provide therapeutic help. To reach them takes time and a trust that has to be painfully won.

People who work in palliative care and visit people at the end of their lives remark on how their meetings with people who are dying transform them. With a dying person, we speak more quickly about what really matters, we meet them at a deeper and more personal level. People in situations of weakness frequently allow their barriers to fall more quickly; they seek less to prove themselves or to hide behind masks. They cannot hide their weakness. There is greater honesty in the way they share and react to things. And the truth sets us free.

Several years ago now, I was invited to give a retreat to the Deny people in Fort Simpson in the North West Territories of Canada. It was a powerful experience being with these men and women, some of whom still lived from hunting, their faces rugged with cold, work and long sleigh journeys. My talks were translated phrase by phrase into the Deny tongue. At one point one of them said, 'We will know if you are speaking the truth because our elders have dreams.' I must have passed the dream test, because they invited me to come back! These native people have suffered greatly, not only because of white people taking over their country but also because of missionaries who have seen them as heathen and far from God. These missionaries felt it their duty to make them abandon the Deny rites and symbols in order to adopt the rites and symbols of what they saw as the 'true' religion. Nowadays, fortunately, albeit a little late, we have begun to appreciate that God was present in this people well before the arrival of white people; that they were a profoundly believing and religious people with a deep sense of God, often led by dreams inspired by God. They also have a deep sense of humanity and of the earth. For far too long they have been pushed aside. And yet they have much to teach Western society which has lost the sense of what it means to be human, of the human community and of the earth! Once again, the stone rejected by the builders can become the corner stone. Those who have been looked at with contempt carry within them the elements needed to heal those who have lorded over them. Yes, those in power need the powerless to refind their humanity and humility.

Being open to and available for others

The difficulty with all this is not so much being ready to stop and listen to people who are different. Certainly, we are afraid of meeting people, of becoming vulnerable, even of being abused by them, but we are even more afraid of all the consequences of getting close to them. It is no trifling thing to befriend someone who is poor. It is easy to visit people serving prison sentences. While they are in prison, there are fixed visiting hours and guards who provide protection. It is easy to listen to and chat with the 'inmates', to enter into friendly relationships with them. The problem comes when they leave prison. There is then a 'danger', especially if we have become friends with them, that they may come and visit not at a fixed time but in the middle of the night. Are we prepared to be disturbed like this, and to live all the consequences of the friendship we have offered?

If we give bread to a hungry person who comes knocking at the door, is there not a danger that that person will come back later? Hunger returns quickly, too quickly. Entering into a relationship with somebody in distress is not without consequences, consequences which affect the way we use our time, our availability, the responsibilities we already have, or perhaps simply our psychological and emotional capacity to be close to another person.

There are choices to be made. Are we prepared to arrange our lives in a different way, to give up certain activities or pastimes or superficial friendships, or even work that we enjoy, in order to live in a new way with new relationships? These sacrifices are not easy; they require a new strength. Are they possible without finding new friends, a new community, new brothers and sisters who can give us the necessary support, courage and encouragement? With these new relationships, we discover people who are lonely and in need; we discover their suffering, their cry and their inner beauty. Through them we are led on to a new path where the barriers around the heart begin to fall and we become people of peace and forgiveness. This is the path to which Raphael and Philippe led me, in a completely unexpected way. It is a path of liberation and inner peace, a path of hope.

An inner transformation

For people who are fixed in their work, family, friends, social status and responsibilities, it may not be possible to make big choices involving great changes to the way they live. Obviously, every time they enter into communion with a person who is ill or handicapped, in prison or in an old people's home, it is going to involve certain sacrifices in terms of their free time. But on a deeper level, this communion can bring about a change of heart in terms of values which hitherto seemed essential. So often we are motivated by honour, the desire for promotion and the need to belong to a social group! And the corollary to this is a certain contempt for those the social group rejects: people with handicaps, immigrants, those who belong to another race or ethnic group, men and women in prison. Even if in theory we do not despise them, in practice, by not being concerned for them, we do.

Then we meet and establish communion with someone who is marginalised or from a different social bracket. We may not have much time to give him or her, but we recognise a bond of communion. The discovery of the beauty and suffering of this person whom, until now, we have tended to despise or to ignore, can begin to shake our hierarchy of values and prejudices. We discover that this person, different in many ways, lives values of truth, kindness and simplicity which perhaps we do not. We discover that he, or she, is close to God.

There are people whose lives have been completely transformed by an encounter with a Muslim man or woman really living his or her faith and a life of prayer. Contempt changes into admiration and respect. Similarly, those who make friends with a person with a mental handicap can find themselves on a path of transformation, and feel suddenly shocked and horrified by the law that exists in France and elsewhere that allows a child with a handicap to be aborted in the mother's womb right up until the time he or she is due to be born. The person who in many societies has been seen as a problem to be resolved, a tragedy to be avoided, somebody to be pushed out of the way, is then seen as a source of light and life. The foundations of a certain vision or social hierarchy are disturbed. We discover for the first time the beauty of human beings, of every human being, the beauty of our humanity which defies all hierarchies of race, sex, religion, social class, nationality, power, intelligence and ability. If there is a hierarchy, it is a hierarchy of the heart, of love. And we are not in a position to judge this kind of hierarchy, because it is a secret hidden in each person. It is God's secret.

This communion is an openness of heart. It creates a chink in the armour around our hearts and our defence mechanisms. It opens us up to another world. It leads us to the discovery that we cannot divide up the world according to social hierarchy; that there are not on the one hand good people, and on the other bad. It challenges ideologies and prejudices about class, race and the family.

It shows up the dishonesty of our societies and of social echelons.

Opening our hearts is never easy, especially when we derive our sense of identity from our social, ethnic, religious or national group, and from our place in this group and the group's values. When we do not have enough self-belief and confidence in our own views and feelings about people and social structures and about our mission in life, we tend to use the group's identity to prove our worth or our superiority. It is painful for us to drop our prejudices and befriend someone rejected and excluded by the social group to which we belong.

Communion with the poor, with strangers, is a personal act of the emerging 'I' or 'self'. It is not a group act; it can even be contradictory to the group's vision. It affirms another reality, and other values. It challenges the conviction that belonging to the group and our place in it are what matters most. This conversion, which is an affirmation of our deepest person as independent of the group, can involve anguish. A Russian who tried to make contact with a stranger visiting Moscow in the Stalinist era might have experienced this anguish, as might an American seeking to befriend a Communist at the time when the Communists were being hunted down, or a Catholic who prayed in a Protestant church before Vatican II, or a young person from a group of tough, strong people who befriends a person with a handicap. It would be the same for an individualistic and cynical person, surrounded by cynical friends, who affirmed her desire to follow Jesus, in a church, so as to be more fully herself and attain greater inner freedom. This person becomes immediately suspect. She is no longer seen by the group as a sure friend, someone who can be relied on. She has gone against the current. She has cut herself off from the others, and affirmed or borne witness to a truth other than theirs. She has affirmed the primacy of personal conscience over collective conscience. She has affirmed the personal 'I'.

Welcoming the enemy

The history of humanity is filled with hostility between human beings. It springs from the deep need written into the heart of every man and woman, of every group of human beings, to prove that they are the best, the strongest, the closest to God. It is intrinsic to all forms of competition. There are those who win and those who lose.

The history of humanity is a history of wars and oppression: one people seeks to suppress another, to take its land and reduce it to slavery. Then, in the hearts of the oppressed, hatred and the need for vengeance are born. There is a cry for life and liberty, a desire to suppress the oppressor and those perceived as oppressors. Walls of hatred or walls of depression and the refusal of life rise up. In order for humanity, or each group, organisation or person to break out of this endless circle of competition, rivalry and war, we have to learn how to be reconciled with the enemy. The enemy is the one who wants to suppress another person or group of people in order to have power and control. The enemy wants to suppress the freedom of others and awakens fear and anguish. But we must not condemn groups and people too quickly. Often hatred has been spread through lies and propaganda by those in power, especially if they control the media. It is easy for them to sow seeds of fear and then hatred in people's hearts. In many Lebanese towns and villages, Muslims and Christians used to live side by side. It was the same with people of different ethnic and religious origins in Rwanda, Bosnia and Northern Ireland. Then, for political and military reasons, suspicion and fear were stirred up, and these led to hatred. Paramilitary groups fought out of loyalty to their group; often they were unable to do otherwise. But frequently before the conflict began, there was no hatred in people's hearts; there was only the desire for peace.

People or races may have enemies, but each of us individually can also have an enemy. This is not somebody far away but somebody close to us, within our circle, at work, in our family, neighbourhood or community. This person seems like a threat to our freedom and personal growth, someone who puts us down, pushes us aside, contradicts us and makes us feel small, angry, anguished, frightened and depressed. An enemy like this cannot always be named or perceived as such. A possessive mother can stand in the way of her child's freedom to grow. She can become her child's enemy. If we want to progress along the path of openness and universal love, we need to become aware that we have enemies.

In order to grow towards inner healing, we need to realise that we are wounded, sick in our hearts and in our relationships with others. We need to become aware of the shadows within us. Similarly, in order to walk towards peace and reconciliation, we need to become aware that we have enemies, and to identify them.

Who are the people we hate, whom we seek at all costs to avoid, whom we find it hard to forgive, who awaken in us feelings of uneasiness, fear and anger which can turn into hatred? During a retreat, a woman once admitted to me that her enemy was her husband. 'He is happy when he can use me for all the household chores,' she said, 'cooking, washing, looking after the children, even sex. But he never listens to me; he does not respect my intelligence or point of view. I feel terrible anger toward him rising up in me.

I don't know what to do with all this anger.' Perhaps for the husband, his wife was the enemy, but he did not dare or was unable to recognise it. Another woman, a young university student, confessed to me that she hated her father. He was a professor of philosophy in a Catholic college, highly thought of in church circles, admired as a good, honest and religious man. 'When he comes home,' the girl told me, 'he shuts himself up in his room to read his books. He never talks to me and never listens to me. I hate him!'

I have already mentioned the system of defence that a child develops in reaction to broken communion. This system leads to a division of humanity into the good and the bad, into friends and enemies.

And then, one day, when the time is ripe, there is a kind of awakening, a new feeling, a desire for change. The spectacle of horrible conflicts and wars, hatred, oppression and death, awakens in us a desire to work for peace in our own surroundings. Things must change! There has been enough conflict. And then maybe we can dare to ask ourselves a question. Is the problem in fact in me? Should I see a psychologist, a priest, or a therapist of some sort? We have a feeling that the enemy is in fact within us. So what should we do now? This is the moment to talk to someone about the people whom we hate, fear or avoid, and to discover, in talking about them, some logic or pattern in our attitude. In some women, for example, there is a fear of men; they give in to them too easily. Other people often seek to fall into the role of victim, accusing others. For some men, women are the enemy because they reveal the chaos within themselves. Some people have a need to control or dominate, a fear of being weak or insecure; the enemy then is the one who says 'No'. For others, authority is the enemy, because they have had bad experiences with their parents. Then a desire for truth and freedom is born, a desire to break the pattern, no longer to avoid or to live in fear of others, or to need to be superior or a victim. It is a desire to become ourselves, no longer to be controlled by past fears or wounds. It is a moment of grace and light. From it is born the desire for reconciliation and peace. Who can change our hearts of stone, hardened by fear, into hearts of flesh so that we can become vulnerable before others? How can our enemies become our friends?

Can the impossible become possible?

In order to respect, welcome and love others, we must first recognise our common humanity and the fact that every human being – the weak and poor as much as the strong and rich – is important and unique. Without this vision and conviction as a foundation, it is impossible to have true moral strength, or to progress towards unity and peace. And, because of this belief in the preciousness of human life, we should also be full of hope. Wounded as they are, human beings are not condemned to division, oppression and hatred. In humanity as a whole, just as in the human body and in the universe, there are powers of healing and balance which allow life to flow. There are men and women, spritual guides, witnesses of love, prophets of peace and reconciliation, who can help people rediscover their source in the God of peace. These men and women are rooted in a vision of faith; and in the call of humanity to unity. They can enable other human beings to struggle for peace and reconciliation and to seek to resolve conflict.

The process of reconciliation with an enemy, the transformation of the person we despise into someone we respect and listen to, often begins with this vision of faith and trust, and in the conviction that there is a divine power hidden in the heart of every human being which urges humanity towards unity and peace. But to advance, we need to be determined, to make definite efforts and to struggle not to be overcome by fear, depression and apathy. These efforts, which constitute forgiveness, begin with our refusal to wish that the enemy might be wiped out, die or disappear, and the recognition that he has a right to exist and live because he is a human being with a heart and feelings. He has a right to a place in the world. He has the right to be himself, with his limitations and poverty, and with his gifts. This acknowledgment implies definite gestures: not speaking badly of him or seeking to put him down. The enemy awakens our fears and blockages, we do not like his way of thinking, we feel no sympathy for him. But this does not diminish the fact that he has a right to be and to live, to have his place, to be able to grow, evolve, change. And at the same time, we need to learn to think kindly about him, to believe that there is some good in him. The struggle to forgive consists in seeing, thinking and believing that there are good things about him, and not constantly looking at what is negative.

We then need to make an effort to understand the enemy in terms of his background, his wounds, his particular fragility, we need to turn the judgment which leads to anger and hatred into understanding and then compassion. The girl who hated her father needed to discover that her father had probably been terribly hurt by his own father. The way he ignored his daughter was the result of these hurts. If one day the girl understood this, then her anger could gradually be transformed into compassion.

Some time ago now, I was in a monastery. In the monastery refectory, talking was not allowed. In front of me there was a very well dressed woman of about fifty-five. She ate like a pig! As I watched her, feelings of irritation and anger welled up in me. Why did she, and the way she ate, have this effect on me? I realised that I had a problem. And, seeing that it was disturbing my peace, I tried to understand it. This woman was clearly anguished and suffering. The way she ate was surely the result of anguish. And so, within myself, I was able to turn judgment and rejection into compassion.

The process of transforming the enemy into someone whom we respect and accept takes time, effort and discipline. Peace does not drop out of the sky. Certainly, it comes from a hidden force of God, but it comes also through the thousand efforts which we make daily, efforts to accept others just as they are, to forgive them, to accept ourselves also, with all our wounds and fragility, to discover that the enemy is within us, to discover also how to cope with our wounds, fears and anguish, and use them in a positive way.

I am touched by the Community of Reconciliation in Corrymeela in Northern Ireland. Founded by a Presbyterian minister, its aim is reconciliation between Catholics and Protestants fighting one another in Ireland. It might for example welcome for a weekend fifteen Catholic mothers who have had a son or husband killed by the Unionist paramilitaries, and fifteen Protestant mothers who have had a son or husband killed by the IRA. These thirty mothers cry, pray and share their suffering together. They discover a path towards peace and reconciliation.

A l'Arche assistant whom I accompany told me about his desire to forgive his father who was very controlling and dominant, and had caused him great suffering. I encouraged him to work towards reconciliation, and I even suggested that they might meet. 'No,' the assistant said to me, 'it's too soon. I am still too fragile and insecure. My father is a strong man who is not good at listening. I need to

235

be stronger within myself before I meet him. If I went to see him today, I would be in danger of being crushed by him. In several years, it might be possible.' I admired this young man's wisdom. Internally, he had experienced forgiveness and reconciliation, but he needed to wait for the fullness of forgiveness, and for this they both needed time. The son needed to become stronger internally, and the father to become a little weaker before he was able to pay attention to his son. Forgiveness is not something that happens in one go. It is a process which takes time. Conflict sprang from the father's wounds and the wounds and fragility of the son. Time was needed to come to terms with these wounds.

A young woman, imprisoned because a man had borne false witness against her, lived a deep conversion following an experience of God. The nun who had been instrumental in her conversion talked to her one day about forgiving this man. 'I cannot,' she said, 'he has hurt me too much.' However she added, 'But I pray every day that God will forgive him.' Sometimes people have suffered too much. They cannot feel forgiveness, but nor do they seek vengeance. They want those who have committed injustice to rediscover truth and justice, to rediscover God, to recognise their faults and sinfulness. Jesus, nailed to the cross, cried out, 'Father, forgive them, for they know not what they do.' Many people who commit murders or abuse children do not know what they are doing. We can pray, however, that somehow they may discern the evil forces in them and change.

The Gospel offers us a commandment from Jesus, 'I say to you, love your enemies, speak well of those who speak badly of you, do good to those you hate, pray for those who persecute you.' These words, spoken to the Galileans persecuted by the Romans, must have seemed shocking.

'How can we love these brutes?' they must have asked themselves, 'these godless people?' And Jesus insisted, 'It is easy to love those who love you, even those who do not believe in God do as much. Truly I say to you love your enemies . . .' Clearly, none of us can love those who abuse us, put us down and push us aside. But these words of Jesus are also a promise. It is as if he were saying, 'I know that you, on your own, cannot forgive. The other person has hurt you too much. But if you want, I will give you a new strength to do what is impossible. I will give you my Spirit, but only if you want it.' It is important not to close ourselves in a static attitude of victimisation, full of hatred, anger and desire for vengeance, but to open our hearts to the spirit of Jesus who slowly heals our blockages and fears, and helps us to make efforts that will set us out along the road to peace.

Resolving conflict

Today, there is an urgent need for us all to learn to resolve conflicts: conflicts in families, between men and women, between parents and children, at work, in organisations and communities, conflicts between countries, races, religions and ethnic groups. Sadly, between the parties concerned there is often brokenness and blockages, as a result of which walls of judgment, prejudice and even hatred have grown up. In conflicts, there are so often the obvious winners and the losers. Sometimes, especially when the winning is through the use of brute force and power, it is the winner who becomes the loser. The guilt and dishonesty hidden in the heart cause a downfall later. Here are a number of principles in this area that I have discovered in my years at l'Arche:

– Never run away from an enemy or a conflict. When the time seems right, try to confront them. Do not, out of fear of facing up to it, minimise the conflict or pretend that it is not that serious. A little fire is easy to extinguish. When it has become a great blaze it is more difficult. A conflict, like a crisis, is evidence of life. It can pave the way for a new time of peace and unity. A conflict that is hidden and denied, which turns into sadness, depression and inner death, is more dangerous than a conflict that is out in the open. But even the latter kind of conflict needs to be taken seriously.

– Listen. Listen to people, to each person, and try to understand what they are saying. Try to understand their point of view, and the wounds that they carry. Listen too to those in authority, those in power, and try to understand the areas in which they are afraid of being challenged. Often those in power are on the defensive.

– Try to distinguish between what is objective and what subjective, to discover where a conflict is the result of some external reality between people of opposing views and beliefs, and where it arises from a clash of personalities. In discord, there are elements that are subjective and emotional, and elements that are objective. In resolving a conflict, we need to try to know both aspects. When one of the parties has a compulsive need to win and extend his or her sphere of influence, we need to make sure that conflict is resolved in such a way that neither loses face. Each side needs to feel that it has gained something and to discover that it is more profitable to co-operate than to fight. If not, one or other will continue fighting.

It takes time to understand the objective elements in a conflict because often two parties use the same words to mean different things. The conflicts between the different Christian churches are not just emotional. They are also

based on different approaches to theology and interpreta-
tions of the Bible. Time is required to understand the other
church's position, their point of view and the reason why
they place so much stress on particular aspects.

This is why, in a community, it is good to have a charter
which sets out the vision, aims and spirit of the community
and a constitution which lays down the way in which the
community is governed. If everybody is in agreement on
these fundamental points, then there is a point of reference
which enables people to move forward together.

– There are conflicts which arise from terrible insecurity
in a person. This insecurity has sometimes been contained
through a role, possessions – sometimes the possession or
control of another person – rigid convictions and religious
rites or particular activities. Take these props away, and
there is an explosion of anguish. The insecurity, or the
inner emptiness, is too much to bear. The person has
not sufficient inner strength to channel her anguish or
feeling of guilt. She needs these external supports which
help her to hide it. A person who experiences the loss of
some responsibility or activity can become extraordinarily
violent towards another, or herself.

But, if people feel sufficiently listened to and respected,
and if they allow others who are competent to help them in
their anguish, this explosion can provide the opportunity for
healing. If they refuse help, they are in danger of struggling
madly to regain whatever it was they depended on to calm
their anguish. Sometimes people like this vacillate between
the role of 'saviour' of an institution or community or
others, and the role of victim, which strangely enough
seems to give them a certain status, and to make it possible
for them to blame and accuse others. It is as if they cannot
accept that they are like other people, with their wounds

and fragilities and limitations, and that it is all right to be like that; they do not have to be the best and perfect.

– Many conflicts arise from the fact that people have different expectations. If we expect something from somebody, and this other person does not deliver it, we feel let down and angry. But if the other was not aware of what was expected, or did not agree with it, then there will be a conflict. Contracts between people are important in avoiding conflict. Often we do not like having contracts. We want to leave things hazy, to remain on a spiritual and emotional level. We are afraid of rationality and law; we are afraid of being precise about what we want or expect. So we refuse to place ourselves on the level of justice or of people's rights and responsibilities.

Generally speaking, many conflicts resolve themselves when both parties can express themselves freely, together, in a secure atmosphere. When they are able to listen to one another and express their more objective needs and expectations calmly, then peace is often possible. For this to happen, competent facilitators or moderators accepted by both parties are sometimes needed.

There are, however, people who seem to refuse all compromise. Their priorities and prejudices are too firmly rooted. They refuse to admit that there is any good in another. They refuse to discuss and are incapable of suspending some of their convictions in order to listen to the other. They have to be the winners or else they will become victims, full of hatred and the desire for vengeance. In this kind of situation, both great patience and great wisdom are needed to keep the hope of change alive.

Today, when there is so much division, it is important that there should be men and women trained in the resolution of conflict, who have the spiritual strength and wisdom needed to listen to opposing sides, to ascertain what it is that can unite them until the fears and prejudices begin to fall and each finds the help needed to take a step towards the other. It is important that there should be more and more places which teach the ways of peace and of approaching conflict and attempting to resolve it. We need even to teach these ways to children in schools. Our world is becoming more and more a place of violence and conflict, and we need to know how to take our place in this world and not run away from it.

We need to recognise, however, that there are some conflicts between people that cannot be resolved. Two sides may have hurt each other too much; they provoke too much fear and anguish in one another. They are unable to admit their own woundedness. The only solution then is a separation which can give each side the space and the time to refind inner peace, and to reflect quietly.

Reproaching people

At l'Arche, I have gained some insight into the art of reproaching people. When we are in a position of authority and responsibility for others it is sometimes necessary to reproach a person who has behaved badly, whether through ignorance, bad temper or ill will. There are anti-social or provocative acts that we cannot ignore, otherwise there is a risk that they will get worse. And, more or less consciously, the person behaving badly is waiting to be confronted and given parameters within which to act. Here are a few comments on the subject:

– Always avoid reproaching people out of your own anger and woundedness; wait until you are in a peaceful state. In one house in Trosly, for example, it had been decided that Pierre should be responsible for waking up the rest of the house and making breakfast at seven o'clock. At half past seven, the person in charge of the house turned up. Pierre was not there, the breakfast was not made and everybody was still in bed. Furious, the person in charge went upstairs to Pierre's room, banged on the door and shouted angrily. But perhaps Pierre had been ill in the night. It would have been better to wait peacefully and then, at a good moment, to ask with tenderness what had happened. Above all, it is better to ask for explanations than to hurl accusations. We need, first of all, to be sure of the facts and the reasons behind them.

– Never reproach somebody without first having let them know that you appreciate and love them. If they have the impression that you reject them and think them worthless, it makes it much harder for them to take criticism. And what is wanted is not to humiliate people but, on the contrary, to help them to grow and do better in future.

– It is good to indicate to the person that you yourself also make mistakes. Then you are not talking from a position of superiority. You are a brother or sister who also has faults and who wants to help the other to grow because you love him or her and believe that he or she has much to give.

– At the heart of all this must be a deep-rooted confidence and belief in these people whom you are reproaching, and a desire to help them to grow positively towards greater liberty, to become more understanding and more true, to discover their capacity for doing good as well as their wounds and particular difficulties.

Non-violence

Non-violence is an attitude when faced with a person, or a group of people, who are aggressive or who oppress others. It is an attitude where we do not hate or want to use violence, but where we want the oppressor to change and to grow in justice and truth. Non-violence is a response to violence, aimed at awakening the oppressor's self-awareness. It is important in all conflict, and particularly when we feel we must confront an enemy. It means allowing our own power of aggression to be tempered with love of those who oppress and with the conviction that they are not totally bad, that there is good in them and that they can change. It means desiring life, not death. Violence as a response to violence is usually the result of fear arising from our own wounds: we need to defend ourselves, or to attack, in order to avoid being crushed. Non-violence, meanwhile, is borne out of love. People like Gandhi, Martin Luther King, Dorothy Day, Jean and Hildegarde Goss-Mayr and many others developed not only a spirituality and philosophy of non-violence but also the tactics necessary to make non-violence work in oppressive political and social situations.

I was close to an example of non-violent action in Brazil in 1974. I was invited with Robert and Nadine, who later founded l'Arche communities in Haiti and Honduras, to the Canadian consulate in San Paolo for dinner with Alphonse Perez, Hildegarde Goss-Mayr and Mario Calvario of Jesus, three witnesses to non-violence. It was a fascinating evening (even though I was almost dropping with exhaustion!). The following morning the Canadian priest with whom Robert, Nadine and I were staying had a telephone call from Mario

Calvario's wife. Her husband had not come home that night after the dinner and she thought he had been arrested. After several telephone calls, the priest confirmed that her suspicions were justified; her husband and the other two had been arrested. After dinner, they had gone back to the airport to look for their luggage which had come in another plane from Buenos Aires. The luggage was full of literature about non-violence. They were then taken to prison where for many hours they underwent interrogation accompanied by psychological torture: screams, threats and so on. At about four o'clock in the morning, the three were reunited. A guard brought them some coffee. They decided to fast and pray for their torturers. At about three o'clock in the afternoon, they were released as a result of pressure from Cardinal Arns who had alerted all the embassies and newspapers. A little later, we met Mario Calvario of Jesus at his house and he told us about what had happened during the night.

I have not myself had any direct experience of non-violence as an instrument in political or social affairs. Its success depends upon the mobilisation of the media, and the support of many people putting pressure on the oppressor. I have, on the other hand, had some experience of non-violence as a means of easing violence in people, above all in people with handicaps whom we have welcomed to l'Arche from psychiatric hospitals. For some, violence is a cry for attention in front of oppression and rejection, an attention they need in order to feel that they exist. It springs from anguish and from a broken self-image. It is often a sign of life and hope. If attention is paid to the person in a positive and welcoming way, responding to violence not with violence but with gentleness and understanding, the violence very often disappears.

Once, I was accosted in the road in Trosly by a large,

strong man from the village. He was completely out of his mind. He hurled abuse at l'Arche, at people with handicaps, whom he hated, and at me, whom he also seemed to hate. He shook his fist, and tried to frighten me. He succeeded. I was terribly frightened, and could feel my heart beating furiously. But at the same time, I could not run away. It was as if I was rooted to the spot. He clouted me on the ear, but not so hard as to knock me to the ground, as he easily could have done. I heard myself say, 'You can hit me again if you want to.' He looked at me, flabbergasted. There was a silence, and then he took me by the hand and invited me into his house. I was shaking, but I followed him. I had been terribly frightened, but through some strength from outside myself, I was able to stand firm and not show my fear. It was he who gave in.

I am not saying that a man intent on killing will always cave in before non-violence. There are so many different kinds of people with different forms of violence in them. All I know is that if a violent person is treated like a human being rather than a wild animal, there is a chance that he will respond like a human being. This means not making him frightened, and trying to talk to him like a human being. But not being frightened, and not making others frightened is not a question of will. It is made possible by that strength which comes from outside, that 'higher power' of which Alcoholics Anonymous speak.

Resolving conflict on the political plane

In so many conflicts or situations where there is oppression, violence erupts because for years and years the oppressor refuses to listen or discuss things. Violence is the language people adopt when they are pushed down, refused justice and not treated as human beings. It is the same in individual situations. A friend with a mental illness was in a psychiatric hospital near Paris. In the course of a visit, I asked him whether he had seen the psychologist, and whether it was difficult to get to see her. He smiled and replied: 'I know how to arrange it. I make a scene, I become violent, and immediately she appears.' Violence is a language, a call, a cry.

In so many political conflicts, where violence breaks out, it is the violence that forces the oppressor to the peace table. South Africa is an example of a people who had to pass through violence (with the support of international powers), in order to achieve democracy and peace. In South Africa they also needed many men and women, prophets of peace, who dared to act without violence, using legal means to weaken the will of the oppressors. In other situations of violence, however, cries for freedom have been crushed with further violence: the natives of Haiti and of the Dominican Republic all died of illnesses that came from Europe, or at the hands of the Spanish and French armies. The Australian Aborigines have been irremediably hurt by white invaders.

The walls separating groups weaken when men and women recognise their common humanity. Prejudices begin to fall away and truth is proclaimed. Enemies begin to listen to one another because they have discovered a reality greater than the victory of one or other party. They have discovered the beauty of each human being, whatever their culture, race or handicaps, and the beauty of co-operation between people.

From the stars to the mud

Human life passes through very different stages on the way from weakness to weakness, from the mother's womb to the womb of the earth. We pass through phases of activity and light, and phases of loss of activity and light, in other words, of suffering. Small children live in the present moment, in a relationship where the flesh and the body are of primary importance. It is a time of relationship, of heart to heart, communicated through the body. It is a time of playing, laughing and the celebration of love. It is a time of communion in trust and simplicity. Later, during adolescence, comes the time of separation from the parents. Life urges the child forward. He has been wounded in his experiences of communion and love. He grows, he searches for the light and becomes suspicious of relationship with his parents. He looks for an identity different from theirs. It is a time of searching for an ideal and for friends, of needing to prove himself, a time of formation. He wants to do things better than his parents. He wants, by himself, to find a new way. He moves towards the universal and the ideal, naively confident (but also uncertain and anxious) of his potential and the potential and worth of the group he moves in. He leaves the smallness of the nest in his desire for greatness and success.

In seeking excellence, recognition and power in a competitive way, he can hurt others. Without necessarily wishing to, he tends to create division, to reinforce the double world of strong and weak, winners and losers, rich and poor, those who are successful and those whose lives seem a failure.

And then there comes a time when he puts down roots. He commits himself to others either in a family or community, and together they discover how they can give life. From the ideal, he comes down to earth. He comes to see how, in searching too much on his own, he has helped to create division. In living daily with others, he discovers his own wounds and fundamental fears. He wants to find peace within himself, to be an instrument of peace and reconciliation in his own life, in his family, in the people around him, his country, his church, between churches and the world. Division, often founded on prejudice and fear, leads to injustice, war, hatred and death. Is there not a way towards unity and peace where each person, whatever his gifts, limitations and weakness can find his place and live? It is then that he discovers that the path to peace does not consist in climbing towards the light in a search for power, recognition and greater and greater influence. The path to peace is in the descent towards people as they are with all their limitations and weaknesses.

An adolescent often runs away from his body and heart. He is afraid of communion, just as he is afraid of chaotic sexual urges within himself. He needs to find himself and his true identity, so that gradually, as an adult, he will be able to feel at ease again with his body and heart, and rediscover relationships of communion and compassion through acts of humility and tenderness. The communion and tenderness he has run away from as an adolescent become the very things he needs in order to rediscover inner unity and to give life. It is a conversion and change of direction. God and universal truth are not in the sky and the stars, nor in theories, ideologies and ideals. They are hidden in actual people, in flesh, mud and matter. They are hidden in the poor and the weak who cry above all for recognition and communion.

Just as some of the purest and most cleansing substances come from things that are rotten – wine and alcohol from fermented fruit, penicillin from mould – and just as the earth is nourished by animal manure, so our hearts and inner brokenness are healed through communion with all that we have rejected and are afraid of: the poor and weak, enemies, strangers. Thus we come down to earth, to the dirt of reality. Because hidden in this earth is a light. This descent is made in humility (a word which comes from the Latin 'humus', meaning earth).

Thus we discover that we need one another. We are part of a common humanity, a universal body in which every individual is important and has a place. We are not made to be solitary heroes, 'admirable' people, but to be fully and profoundly human, each in his or her place, with his or her gifts and limitations, in the body of humanity. If we forget the 'earth' of our world, the 'earth' of our bodies and our hearts – if we believe that we are made up simply of desire, intelligence, spirit, self-consciousness and power – then we are heading for disaster. Everything will fall apart if we only want things on a big scale, and if we put ourselves on pedestals and forget people who are small, weak, physically fragile or prone to illness, people who need care, food, rest and friendship. The great temptation for every human being is to be seduced by power and to refuse communion with the vulnerability and littleness it implies. But if we follow the way of the heart and communion with real people, we can rebuild the earth together.

This world is a valley of tears. There is illness and death; there are divisions, hatred, oppression and war; there is injustice and inequality. In every person there is a struggle between war and peace, light and darkness, trust and fear, altruism and egoism, openness and closedness. Faced with suffering, illness, death and weakness, there can be an awakening and a call to love and compassion, just as there can be a flight into ideas and theories and, consequently, into a hardening of the heart.

Coming down to earth means also descending into the murk of our shadow side: our fears, darkness and inner wounds. The conversion from the way of competition to the way of the heart and of communion involves passing through the dark night of anguish and of feelings of guilt. The poor and vulnerable outside us reveal the poverty and vulnerability within us. If we are to discover true communion, in which we do not possess other people, we will have to undergo a kind of death in which we learn to trust and abandon ourselves. But it is a particular kind of abandonment. We cannot truly abandon ourselves unless we accept that we are loved by God, freely and unconditionally, in the murkiness and deep poverty of our being, in our helplessness and guilt. This is the first and ultimate revelation. We do not need to defend ourselves. We are forgiven and loved. In discovering this, we return silently to the source, to peace, to communion and inner ecstasy. God dwells within us. He is no longer a shining presence in the heavens, but a humble presence in the mud of our inner being.

Humanity today is at a cross-roads. Technology enables us to do everything, except to bring people together in love and thus make our world a happier and more loving place. Technology alone brings material progress. It gives power. It takes us some way towards conquering the moon and stars. Is it not now time to come back down to earth, to rediscover the beauty of our earth, of humanity, of each one of us? Then we can reach out together to the weak and the poor, using all that is good and humane in technology, so that our hearts and intelligence can be transformed through compassion.

But this return to earth, to humanity, to a new form of solidarity where walls disappear, to communion with each person, demands a conversion. What can bring this about? How can we begin to change our world, one heart at a time?

How can we set out on this journey home? How can we discover that light and healing are found in those things we have hidden behind walls, that we despise and reject as dirty, ugly and strange? What experience of light, love and inner peace is needed to bring about this change in attitude? In the Book of Hosea, there is a text that can help us. Writing in the seventh century before Christ, the prophet offers us these words of God, 'This is why I am going to allure her. I am going to lead her out into the desert and I am going to talk to her heart. And I will change the Valley of Achor into a door of hope' (Hosea 2: 14–15).

The Valley of Achor (which signifies the valley of misery) was a deep and notoriously dangerous gorge near Jericho. The Hebrew people avoided and circumvented it. It was a hideout not only for brigands, but also wild animals, snakes and scorpions. And then Hosea announces that God, in a loving encounter, will speak to our hearts and turn this valley into a gateway of hope. It will no longer be a place to be avoided. If we dare enter it, we will discover that it leads to life. If, after an experience of God's tenderness, we can dare enter the world of our own darkness, where our demons lurk, and enter also the world of suffering and poverty around us and in us, then we will be liberated from our fears. No longer will we need to run away into the stars, into power and into 'superiority'. We will become messengers of hope.

MARQUIS

PRINTED BY
IMPRIMERIE D'ÉDITION MARQUIS
IN FEBRUARY 1997
MONTMAGNY (QUÉBEC)